THE
GOOD
QUALITY
MANAGER'S
GUIDE

*checklists for practical
quality management*

TREVOR BOUTALL

Request for Comment

We would like to know what you think of this guide and how you are using it. We are particularly interested to know of any way in which its content, language, style or layout could be improved so that it would better meet your needs.

Please send your comments to: MCI, Russell Square House, 10-12 Russell Square, London WC1B 5BZ.

Acknowledgements

Thanks to Penny Foxton, Karen Marshall, Joe McCullagh, Beryl Nelms for contributing to the text and production of this guide.

Thanks also to the thousands of managers who tested drafts of the checklists.

Copyright

Published by the Management Charter Initiative, the operating arm of the National Forum for Management Education and Development, Russell Square House, 10-12 Russell Square, London WC1B 5BZ. Registered Charity No. 1002554.

The Good Quality Manager's Guide

ISBN 1 897587 27 9

Contents

How to use this guide	**5**
Quality Management	**7**
What is Quality Management?	8
Developing a Quality Culture	13
Promoting the Importance of Quality	15
Promoting Quality in Organisational Plans	19
Supporting Your Organisation's Quality Vision	23
Supporting Quality Policies and Strategies	25
Supporting Quality Processes and Systems	29
Assuring Quality	33
Supporting Quality Measurement	35
Evaluating Quality	39
Supporting Continuous Improvement	43
Operational Management	**47**
What is Operational Management?	48
Managing the Operation	51
Meeting Customer Needs	53
Managing Change	59
Quality Assurance	65
Time Management	67
Managing People	69
Personnel Planning	71
Developing Teams and Individuals	77
Managing Teams and Individuals	85
Working Relationships	91
Managing Problems with Staff	97
Equal Opportunities	101
Managing Finance	105
Managing Budgets	107
Cost Control	111
Managing Information	113
Using Information	115
Meetings	121

National Standards   **125**

What are National Standards?   126

National Vocational Qualifications   128

Standards for Managing Quality   130

Middle Management Standards   132

Links between the Checklists and the Standards   134

Keywords Index   **137**

Useful Addresses   **143**

How to use this guide

Quality management is about helping your organisation consistently to meet customer requirements and continuously to improve its performance. Whether you are a full-time quality manager or a general manager who has special responsibility for quality management, you will find this book describes what you have to do. Knowing what you have to do is the essential first step to being effective.

As a quality manager, you are often required to perform a number of functions simultaneously for which you need a wide repertoire of skills and a broad suite of technical knowledge as well as common sense. You are required to respond to new developments and fast-changing circumstances, and to work at many different levels.

The Good Quality Manager's Guide breaks down the quality manager's role into simple, practical checklists to help you tackle quality management tasks successfully. There is no magic in it, just crystal clear objectives and strictly logical steps.

The checklists can be used for a variety of purposes, such as job descriptions, recruitment, appraisal schemes and performance management. However, they are designed, first and foremost, to help you do your job. Here are some examples of how you might use them.

Addressing unfamiliar tasks

You may be faced with a task you have not performed for a long time, or perhaps never met before. Take developing a quality policy for your organisation, for example. How would you go about it?

The contents page tells you that, under *Supporting Your Organisation's Quality Vision*, there is a section on *Supporting Quality Policies and Strategies*. There are 2 checklists to help you. *Supporting the development of quality policies* helps you advise management on how to develop and communicate policies which lead to quality. *Identifying strategies to implement quality policies* will help you identify and select the most appropriate and effective strategy.

> **Contents**
> ▶ Supporting Your Organisation's Quality Vision
> ▶ Supporting Quality Policies and Strategies
> ▶ 2 checklists

Tackling important tasks

You may have to do something critically important which you want to ensure you get right – running an important meeting for instance.

Keywords Index
▶ Meetings
▶ Leading
▶ Leading meetings

The keywords index at the back of the book points to the checklist for *Leading meetings*. This helps ensure you get the best from all participants, arrive at well-informed decisions and get there in the fastest possible time.

Checking that you are doing things properly

Identifying your customers' quality requirements may be something you do on a regular basis but you may like to check occasionally that you are doing things properly.

Keywords Index
▶ Customers
▶ Requirements
▶ Identifying customers' quality requirements

The keyword index shows there is a checklist on *Identifying customers' quality requirements* for quality managers as well as a more general checklist on *Establishing and agreeing customer requirements* in the *Operational Management* section.

Carrying out a public task

Some aspects of quality management are more public than others, so it is important not just to get it right, but to be seen to get it right.

Contents
▶ Developing a Quality Culture
▶ Promoting the Importance of Quality
▶ 2 checklists

For example, *Promoting the Importance of Quality* requires consultation with key people at many different levels, helping them to understand the benefits of quality and the particular role they can play. There are 2 checklists to help you: *Promoting the strategic role of quality* and *Promoting quality throughout your organisation*.

You should find checklists to cover all your quality management tasks. They are based on the national Standards for Managing Quality developed by the Management Charter Initiative (MCI). If you can prove you are competent in the areas covered by the checklists, you could qualify for units towards a National (or Scottish) Vocational Qualification. Refer to pages 128-129.

Quality
Management

What is Quality Management?

The key purpose of quality management is to enhance the organisation's capability to improve its performance and develop excellence for its customers.

Meeting customer requirements and continuous improvement in the quality of the organisation's services and products are responsibilities shared by all who work for the organisation. The checklists for quality management are therefore relevant to a wide range of people, including:

- senior managers who must develop policies and strategies for assuring quality and, through their leadership, motivate everyone to achieve excellence
- those who have a specific remit for quality management, with job titles such as Quality Manager, Quality Director, Quality Consultant or Quality Engineer
- those whose role includes the task of installing or maintaining a quality system or programme as part of a wider management role
- those who have a line management or functional role which includes some responsibility for quality control, assessment, auditing or inspection.

However the responsibility is shared, it is important that all involved understand what their role is and what is expected of them. Many managers do not have full responsibility for quality management and may find specific checklists are useful to help them tackle the functions which have been delegated to them. Those with a wider remit for quality management as a whole will find the checklists fully cover their role.

Quality management in its broadest sense is about providing expert advice and guidance, at all levels in the organisation, to develop systems and procedures that will ensure customer requirements are met on time, every time. It is also about identifying trends and developments both within the organisation and in the wider environment and recommending ways in which services, products and processes can be improved.

An important aspect of quality management is developing a culture of quality and continuous improvement which runs through the bloodstream of the organisation. This requires gaining the commitment of senior management to defining quality as the central force in the organisation's strategies and promoting quality and its benefits throughout the organisation. As a manager with responsibility for quality, you may find you have a key role to play in accurately defining customer requirements, assessing your organisation's ability to meet them and advising on the improvements necessary.

On a practical level, quality managers have to provide senior management with advice on developing policies which will support the vision of quality and recommend strategies by which they can be implemented. Line managers will also require practical advice on how they can develop the most effective, healthy and safe working environments, processes and systems to ensure the delivery of quality services and products within organisational guidelines and legal constraints.

As well as providing advice and guidance, quality managers are often called upon to develop or improve systems for measuring quality and to analyse and interpret the information provided. They have to evaluate the quality of services and products and also how effective the systems are to assure consistent quality and identify opportunities for improvements.

An overview of the quality management role is given in the table below.

Developing a Quality Culture	Supporting Your Organisation's Quality Vision	Assuring Quality
Promoting the Importance of Quality Promoting Quality in Organisational Plans	Supporting Quality Policies and Strategies Supporting Quality Processes and Systems	Supporting Quality Measurement Evaluating Quality Supporting Continuous Improvement

At different times quality managers are required to be adviser, consultant, mentor, designer, engineer, implementor, inspector, critic and judge. Quality managers require a considerable depth of technical knowledge and a wide range of skills in order to succeed. These require time, experience and appropriate training to develop effectively. However, the checklists in this book are designed to provide you with some simple, practical checklists to help you tackle quality management tasks effectively.

Apart from your quality responsibilities, you will no doubt also have general management duties to perform. The complementary section on Operational Management is full of checklists to help you succeed in your wider management role.

You will find the checklists in this book useful whether your organisation has formal systems for quality assurance, such as BS EN ISO 9000 or Investors in People, informal systems developed in-house to meet your organisation's specific requirements or no systems at all – but a clear need to develop appropriate systems. The principles of good quality management are the same whatever title or kitemark the initiative is given.

BS EN ISO 9000

Probably the most common quality system is BS EN ISO 9000 (formally known as BS 5750). It requires the development of systems which clearly define what is being done in the organisation. It demands appropriate measurements and controls to ensure that services and products which do not meet specified standards are rejected before they reach the customer.

The checklists in this book describe what a quality manager has to do in order to create a quality system accredited to BS EN ISO 9000. They also go beyond this to meet the Total Quality Standard BS 7850.

UK Quality Award/European Quality Award

The British Quality Award and the European Quality Award have identical criteria (divided into *enablers* and *results*) for measuring the performance of the organisation as a whole. They cover all aspects of an organisation's operations, its customers and suppliers and are intended to lead to Total Quality Management in its broadest definition. The checklists in this book will help you make tangible improvements against the nine criteria in the European TQM model.

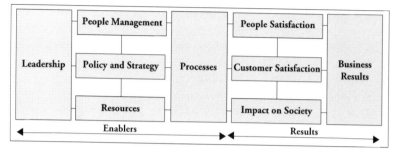

Figure: *European TQM Model*

Investors in People

Investors in People is a national standard, the key purpose of which is *to achieve objectives and continuously improve performance by investing in people.* Its four principles involve commitment, planning, action and evaluation in order to empower individuals to make a positive contribution to the organisation's performance.

Figure: *The Investors in People national standard*

The checklists in this book can be used to support work towards your goal of becoming an Investor in People. The following table shows which checklists are most useful at each stage in the cycle.

Investors in People Principles	Quality Management Checklists
Commitment	Promoting the Importance of Quality Promoting Quality in Organisational Plans Supporting Quality Policies and Strategies
Planning	Promoting Quality in Organisational Plans Supporting Quality Policies and Strategies
Action	Supporting Quality Policies and Strategies Supporting Quality Processes and Systems
Evaluation	Supporting Quality Measurement Evaluating Quality Supporting Continuous Improvement

Figure: *Links between the Checklists and Investors in People*

Developing a Quality Culture

Developing a Quality Culture is about ensuring that everyone, at both the strategic and operational levels, is committed to meeting customer requirements and striving continuously to improve performance. It involves:

Promoting the Importance of Quality   15

Promoting the strategic role of quality   16
Promoting quality throughout your organisation   17

Promoting Quality in Organisational Plans   19

Identifying customers' quality requirements   20
Assessing your organisation's quality performance   21
Advising on improvements   22

Promoting the Importance of Quality

This section is about getting everyone – senior decision-makers, managers, employees, suppliers, customers and others – to understand the importance and value of quality to the organisation.

The checklists will help you to:

- promote the benefits of quality to decision-makers
- persuade decision-makers to make quality a strategic goal
- identify and seize opportunities to promote quality throughout your organisation.

The process for *Promoting the Importance of Quality* looks like this:

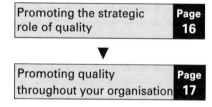

| Promoting the strategic role of quality | Page 16 |

▼

| Promoting quality throughout your organisation | Page 17 |

Promoting the Importance of Quality

Promoting the strategic role of quality

1. **Identify the features of quality such as quality standards, systems and practices** - how relevant are these features to your organisation's vision, mission and values?

2. **Promote the benefits of quality such as customer satisfaction, employee motivation, consistency of supply, accident reduction and cost savings** - help decision-makers understand how quality can support the achievement of strategic goals.

3. **Make a strong case for quality** - present accurate information to decision-makers with the appropriate degree of urgency.

4. **Ask decision-makers for their views** - get decision-makers to share their views of the strategic role of quality and make appropriate responses.

5. **Make the links between quality and your organisation** - seize opportunities to make clear links between quality and the role and function of each part of your organisation.

6. **Publicise improvements made** - support your case for quality by referring to the benefits of any improvements already made.

7. **Offer alternatives** - where your suggestions are not adopted by decision-makers, identify the reasons and make alternative proposals.

Promoting quality throughout your organisation

1. **Look for opportunities to create and sustain awareness of quality** - how relevant are these opportunities in the light of your organisation's vision, mission and values?

2. **Select the best options** - choose those opportunities most likely to maximise the awareness of quality throughout your organisation and its networks.

3. **Provide information on your organisation's vision of quality both internally and externally** - make sure your information is up-to-date and consistent with your organisation's current performance and priorities.

4. **Communicate information positively** - emphasise the way in which quality will contribute to your organisation's success.

5. **Highlight each individual's role in the drive for quality** - encourage people to take responsibility for their own contribution to quality.

6. **Promote the key importance of quality** - emphasise the key role quality plays in the continued improvement and effectiveness of your organisation.

7. **Develop champions** - encourage decision-makers to motivate individuals to be involved in quality improvement.

8. **Find out what others think** - ask people what their views on quality are and make appropriate responses to them.

Developing a Quality Culture

Promoting Quality in Organisational Plans

This section is about making sure your organisation's plans and processes for producing and delivering services and products meet quality requirements.

The checklists will help you to:

- identify and agree with external and internal customers what their quality requirements are

- assess how well your organisation is doing against these requirements and the standards it has set itself

- advise on the improvements to be made.

The process of *Promoting Quality in Organisational Plans* looks like this:

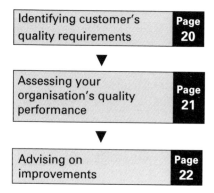

| Identifying customer's quality requirements | Page 20 |

▼

| Assessing your organisation's quality performance | Page 21 |

▼

| Advising on improvements | Page 22 |

Refer also to the checklists on **Managing Change** (pages 59-63) and **Quality Assurance** (pages 65-66) in the section on Operational Management.

Identifying customers' quality requirements

1. **Choose appropriate methods for identifying requirements of internal and external customers** - methods may include surveys, meetings, specifications, contracts, formal and informal feedback.

2. **Provide a detailed analysis** - make sure the outcomes of your analysis are sufficiently detailed for the purpose for which they are required and are supported by the information available.

3. **Draw appropriate conclusions** - make sure your methods provide accurate and comprehensive information, both qualitative and quantitative, which allows you to draw sound conclusions about customer requirements.

4. **Identify customer's requirements and expectations** - check that you have identified these accurately and comprehensively.

5. **Compare your performance with others** - check how your organisation compares with your competitors or with other organisations providing similar services or products.

6. **Agree standards of quality** - agree clear, relevant and assessable standards of quality with customers and present these in appropriate formats, for example in a contract, in terms of business or in a code of business or customer charter.

7. **Check that agreed standards meet organisational requirements** - are they consistent with organisational values and policies; do they comply with relevant legislation (e.g. Health and Safety)?

Promoting Quality in Organisational Plans

Assessing your organisation's quality performance

1. **Obtain information on your organisation's performance** - get accurate and current information from appropriate sources on the quality of your organisation's products, services and processes.

2. **Benchmark your organisation's performance** - how well are you doing compared with your competitors and other organisations providing similar services or products?

3. **Check your organisation's performance complies with legal requirements** - are you meeting minimum legal standards?

4. **Choose appropriate methods of assessment of your organisation's quality performance such as quality inspection, performance reviews and customer feedback** - select or develop methods of assessment which allow information about performance to be interpreted and evaluated against customer requirements.

5. **Identify ways of improving performance** - use assessments as a way of identifying realistic and effective ways in which your organisation can improve its performance.

6. **Evaluate your organisation's quality standards against its vision of quality** - are you performing to the standards that you have set yourselves?

Promoting Quality in Organisational Plans

Advising on improvements

1. **Prioritise improvements** - develop and agree clear, valid and comprehensive criteria, including the assessment of relative risk, to judge which potential improvements have highest priority.

2. **Use appropriate costing and valuing systems** - check that your methods of analysing costs and benefits are appropriate to your organisation.

3. **Undertake detailed cost-benefit analysis** - present the costs and the benefits of improving performance in different activities clearly, so that they can easily be understood.

4. **Assess the cost of quality conformance and quality non-conformance** - there will be a cost to assuring quality, but it may be less than the penalty of providing goods or services which do not meet quality standards or using processes which lead to accidents and downtime. There may also be added value from improving quality.

5. **Avoid obstacles to change** - evaluate any actual or potential obstacles to making the improvements and propose measures to overcome them.

6. **Make clear and comprehensive recommendations** - your recommendations should cover:
   • all the essential actions to be taken
   • likely benefits, such as reduction in costs and accidents, increase in customer loyalty
   • resource implications
   • potential constraints and limiting factors, including legal requirements.

7. **Identify the consequences of changes to your supplier base** - quality improvements may mean that your suppliers need to improve their quality standards or you need to change suppliers. Recommend ways of dealing with these issues in order to minimise disruption to supply.

Supporting Your Organisation's Quality Vision

Supporting Your Organisation's Quality Vision is about providing advice and guidance to senior management on quality policies and strategies and to line management on quality systems and processes. It involves:

Supporting Quality Policies and Strategies   25

Supporting the development of quality policies   26
Identifying strategies to implement quality policies   27

Supporting Quality Processes and Systems   29

Advising on the impact of working environments and
  processes on quality   30
Advising on the implementation of quality systems   31

Quality Management

Supporting Quality Policies and Strategies

This section is about helping senior management develop policies and strategies to support your organisation's quality vision.

The checklists will help you to:

- advise senior management on developing and communicating appropriate and consistent policies to support quality
- help decision makers select strategies which will enable these policies to be implemented effectively
- advise on the implications for teams, individuals, suppliers and customers.

The process of *Supporting Quality Policies and Strategies* looks like this:

| Supporting the development of organisational quality policies | Page 26 |

▼

| Identifying strategies to implement quality policies | Page 27 |

Supporting Quality Policies and Strategies

Supporting the development of quality policies*

1. **Explain the nature and purpose of quality concepts, standards, systems and programmes to policy makers** - provide a clear and accurate explanation.

2. **Provide advice to management on appropriate methods of communicating quality policies.**

3. **Explain the significance of performance measurement to the organisation's success.**

4. **Explain why a documented system for the effective implementation of quality is necessary** - use examples to illustrate the benefits.

5. **Encourage your senior managers to clarify and make explicit their vision of and commitment to quality** - this will help them to develop policies to support your organisation's mission.

6. **Highlight any internal inconsistencies** - if there are inconsistencies in the aims and commitments of senior management, bring these to their attention and suggest ways of resolving these differences.

7. **Highlight any external conflicts** - if your organisation's vision of quality conflicts with the aims of suppliers or customers, look for ways of resolving these conflicts, either through discussion with suppliers and customers or through amendment of your organisation's vision.

* *Policies which have an effect on overall quality may relate to:*
- *design of processes producing services and products*
- *design of processes for delivering services and products*
- *processes and systems within your organisation including documentation*
- *employees, including their training and development*
- *health and safety*
- *customers*
- *supplies and procurement strategies.*

Identifying strategies to implement quality policies

1. **Help decision-makers to identify and select strategies which are consistent with your organisation's vision of quality and with other policies and values** - provide the necessary information, opportunities and support.

2. **Weigh up the options for implementing quality strategies** - what are their advantages and disadvantages, what are the resource implications.

3. **Present your recommendations** - having weighed up the options, present these clearly to decision makers, together with your recommendations.

4. **Clarify the role of suppliers in implementing quality policy** - how important are your suppliers in achieving your agreed quality standards?

5. **Identify strategies to develop your organisation's supplier base** - recommend strategies to develop suppliers which will support your organisation's quality objectives.

Supporting Quality Processes and Systems

This section is about helping your organisation achieve its vision of quality.

The checklists will help you to:

- advise people on developing working environments, processes and systems of control to produce and deliver quality services and products
- advise people to develop and improve quality systems
- gain people's support for developing and maintaining quality systems

The process of *Supporting Quality Processes and Systems* looks like this:

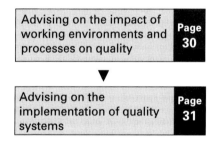

| Advising on the impact of working environments and processes on quality | Page 30 |

▼

| Advising on the implementation of quality systems | Page 31 |

Refer also to the checklist on **Quality Assurance** (pages 65-66) in the section on Operational Management.

Supporting Quality Processes and Systems

Advising on the impact of working environments and processes on quality

1. **Communicate accurate and relevant information about the potential impact of the working environment on meeting quality requirements** - bring this information to the attention of the people concerned. The working environment may include:
    *   premises and workplace
    *   plant and process machinery
    *   materials and operational procedures
    *   health and safety legislation.

2. **Encourage your organisation to develop suitable working environments and systems of control** - these should be appropriate for the activities undertaken and meet the needs of those who work within these environments.

3. **Encourage your organisation to evaluate and improve the working environment, processes and use of resources to meet quality standards.**

4. **Encourage your organisation to keep appropriate documentation and records relating to the working environment** - these should be made available to authorised people when required.

5. **Identify legal requirements** - check on the law regarding workplace conditions, health and safety and consider how it may affect the quality of products, services and processes.

Advising on the implementation of quality systems

1. **Provide information and support** - provide the information and support required to develop quality systems and documentation, including the definition of quality responsibilities.

2. **Assess your organisation's understanding of quality** - does your organisation understand what is required to achieve relevant quality standards and specifications?

3. **Identify your organisation's current quality standards** - what are the quality specifications currently used by your organisation and how are they developed? Use this as an opportunity to develop a relationship with those responsible for developing and working to quality specifications.

4. **Develop implementation plans for quality systems** - agree realistic time schedules and the roles and responsibilities of everyone involved.

5. **Agree monitoring procedures** - agree with those responsible how quality systems are going to be monitored once they have been implemented.

6. **Gain support for quality systems** - use a range of communication and motivational techniques to gain individuals' active support for the development, implementation and monitoring of quality systems.

Assuring Quality

Assuring Quality is about making sure the systems are in place to measure and evaluate quality on a continuous basis and offer recommendations on how the quality of services, products and processes can be improved. It involves:

Supporting Quality Measurement   **35**

Supporting the design and development of quality
measurement systems   36
Supporting the collection, analysis and documentation
of information relating to quality   37

Evaluating Quality   **39**

Designing and implementing evaluation systems   40
Managing information on organisational performance   41

Supporting Continuous Improvement   **43**

Evaluating the quality of products, services and processes 44
Advising on continuous quality improvement   45

Refer also to the checklist on *Quality Assurance* (pages 65-66) in the section on Operational Management.

Supporting Quality Measurement

This section is about helping people develop systems for measuring quality and use them effectively.

The checklists will help you:

- communicate the benefits of quality measurement systems effectively
- encourage and support the development of appropriate systems
- support the collection, analysis and documentation of information

The process of *Supporting Quality Measurement* looks like this

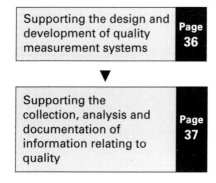

| Supporting the design and development of quality measurement systems | Page 36 |

▼

| Supporting the collection, analysis and documentation of information relating to quality | Page 37 |

Supporting the design and development of quality measurement systems

1. **Identify your organisation's quality standards and current methods for measuring quality performance** - use this as an opportunity to work in partnership with those involved.

2. **Communicate the use and benefits of performance measures and quality measurement tools and techniques** - show people how to incorporate these effectively into the design of systems and processes. Tools and techniques might include:
   - quality planning
   - defining criteria
   - quality evaluation
   - controlling plans
   - investigating quality problems
   - monitoring quality costs
   - costing accidents and downtime.

3. **Encourage individuals to evaluate the effectiveness of your organisation's current performance measures** - give them appropriate information, advice and opportunities.

4. **Encourage individuals to evaluate reports and recommendations from auditors and other sources** - show them how they might use these in designing systems and processes.

5. **Encourage individuals to develop clear and concise criteria for system design and use** - provide the necessary information and opportunities.

6. **Encourage participation, acceptance and correct use of systems** - by clearly explaining the reasons for designing and introducing the systems.

7. **Help individuals collect information on the success of the system in meeting the criteria** - help them put in place a monitoring system which provides regular and timely information.

8. **Think about the people you are supporting** - present information and advice in a way which is appropriate to the person concerned.

Assuring Quality

Supporting the collection, analysis and documentation of information relating to quality

1. **Agree the amount and nature of support required** - discuss and agree requirements with the people concerned.

2. **Provide advice on the application of quality management tools and techniques to the area of work** - make sure your advice is clear, accurate and justifiable.

3. **Provide any necessary documentation** - make available documentation relating to quality management tools and techniques within the timescales you have agreed.

4. **Think about those to whom you are giving support** - provide the support in an appropriate manner and keep sensitive issues confidential.

5. **Encourage feedback** - ask for feedback on the collection, analysis and interpretation of data and provide help where necessary.

Evaluating Quality

This section is about developing systems to evaluate the quality of services and products and using the information provided to measure organisational performance.

The checklists will help you to:

- develop effective and reliable systems for evaluating quality
- get accurate and reliable information on which to base evaluations.

The process of *Evaluating Quality* looks like this

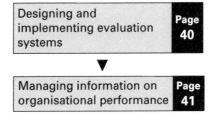

| Designing and implementing evaluation systems | Page 40 |

▼

| Managing information on organisational performance | Page 41 |

Designing and implementing evaluation systems

1. **Establish and agree the objectives and scope of the evaluation** - use this as an opportunity to develop working relationships with the people concerned.

2. **Identify appropriate performance measures and assessment tools and techniques** - these may include tools and techniques for quality planning, defining criteria, evaluating tools, controlling plans, investigating quality problems and monitoring the cost of quality.

3. **Identify and confirm the availability of appropriate sources of information** - you may require information about products, services, processes, customers or suppliers.

4. **Use existing internal information sources** - where they are available and reliable use existing systems rather than establishing new systems.

5. **Identify the resources needed for the evaluation**.

6. **Negotiate where necessary** - where you cannot obtain sufficient resources for the evaluation, modify the objectives and scope of the evaluation with the agreement of the people concerned.

7. **Document your evaluation systems and processes** - check with others that your documentation is clear, accurate and concise.

8. **Communicate effectively** - have you told all the people affected about your evaluation?

9. **Keep accurate and complete records** - and use these to support the continuous improvement of the evaluation system and processes.

10. **Use a sampling approach where appropriate** - but make sure it is justifiable in terms of technique, cost and data likely to be obtained.

Managing information on organisational performance

1. **Validate information** - use an agreed or specified method to validate the information you obtain.

2. **Include information from customers and suppliers** - get information from customers and suppliers on the quality of your products, services and processes.

3. **Get sufficient information** - you need enough information to be able to make an accurate and complete assessment.

4. **Address any problems with the information** - where you identify weaknesses, confusions or discrepancies in the information, investigate and resolve these where possible.

5. **Document and store the information** - record and store both the information obtained and the conclusions of the analysis accurately and completely taking into account legal and organisational requirements.

6. **Encourage people to contribute** - ask people to provide information honestly and openly in the interests of improving quality.

7. **Use the information to help identify areas where standards of quality need to be improved.**

Supporting Continuous Improvement

This section is about supporting continuous improvement by evaluating the quality of products, services and processes and recommending ways of improving them.

The checklists will help you to:

- monitor and evaluate the quality of services, products and processes
- identify problems and take corrective action
- identify the impact of internal and external trends and developments
- recommend and support the implementation of improvements

The process of *Supporting Continuous Improvement* looks like this

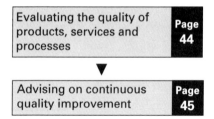

| Evaluating the quality of products, services and processes | Page 44 |

| Advising on continuous quality improvement | Page 45 |

Evaluating the quality of products, services and processes

1. **Monitor and analyse operational information relating to quality** - look for any actual or potential problems.

2. **Get sufficient information** - make sure you have sufficient information to support any decision which you or others may have to make.

3. **Obtain additional information** - where current information is insufficient, or where additional information could improve the evaluation.

4. **Identify the causes of problems** - where products, services, processes or individuals are failing to achieve quality standards.

5. **Take corrective action** - take action quickly where you see actual or potential failure to meet standards.

6. **Keep records of non-conformance** - where products, services and processes do not conform to quality standards, keep accurate, legible and complete records of the problem and assess the overall effect on the area concerned.

7. **Offer appropriate and timely advice** - offer advice to those not meeting quality standards at a time when it is of most use to them and in a way which helps them improve their performance.

8. **Advise management of intractable problems** - where it is not possible to resolve a situation, let management know the problem clearly and accurately.

Advising on continuous quality improvement

1. **Assess the outcomes of continuous monitoring and quality evaluations** - what are the implications for your organisation?

2. **Identify both internal and external trends and developments in the quality of products, services and processes** - gain as much information as possible within cost and time constraints.

3. **Advise on the impact of trends and development** - let people know quickly what the impact of trends and developments may be on the actual or perceived quality of your organisation's products, services and processes.

4. **Make recommendations for improvements** - put forward clear and well-documented proposals for improvements in the quality of products, services and processes.

5. **Do a cost-benefit analysis** - explain the benefits the improvements could bring against the resources needed to effect the improvements.

6. **Think about your audience** - present your proposals in a suitable form which allows people to take decisions.

7. **Offer continuing support where your recommendations for change are agreed**.

8. **Monitor the improvements** - check that they are delivering the expected benefits, within the agreed costs.

Assuring Quality

Operational
Management

What is Operational Management?

The key purpose of management is to achieve the organisation's objectives and continuously improve its performance.

Operational management is being clear about the objectives you have to achieve through your team, in your department or for your part of the business; and using the available resources to best effect.

It involves managing the operation of your part of the organisation as effectively as possible; being clear about what you are expected to deliver; designing systems and procedures; and organising the workplace to achieve this. Always you need to be looking for, and implementing, ways of doing things better to provide a quality service or product every time.

Operational management means getting things done through people. You have to make sure you have the right people to do the job. You have to develop a team and help each member of the team develop the skills they need to perform their job effectively. You need to plan the work and allocate it amongst the team, setting individual objectives and providing feedback on their performance. Managing people involves building effective working relationships and dealing with difficult problems, being careful to be fair and equitable in all your dealings.

As a manager, you will often be required to prepare budgets for the expenditure, and perhaps income, for your part of the operation. It is your responsibility to ensure that these financial targets are met and that all staff are aware of how they can help in improving the financial performance. Operational management also involves obtaining and using information to aid decision-making; and leading and participating effectively in meetings to arrive at decisions.

Operational Management

Managing the Operation	Managing People
Meeting Customer Needs	Personnel Planning
Managing Change	Developing Teams and Individuals
Quality Assurance	Managing Teams and Individuals
Time Management	Working Relationships
	Managing Problems with Staff
	Equal Opportunities

Managing Finance	Managing Information
Managing Budgets	Using Information
Cost Control	Meetings

Operational management is a complex business requiring a range of skills and knowledge, together with disciplined time-management, if you are to succeed. However, the checklists in this book provide some simple, practical guidelines for effectively tackling everyday tasks. You will find them relevant whether you are a team leader, supervisor or manager at any level, although you may find your role is to contribute to, rather than have full responsibility for, an activity.

Managing the Operation

Managing the Operation is about working out ways of meeting customer requirements on time, every time. It involves:

Meeting Customer Needs   53

Establishing and agreeing customer requirements   54
Maintaining supplies   55
Maintaining a productive work environment   56
Meeting customer specifications   57
Solving problems for customers   58

Managing Change   59

Identifying opportunities for improvements   60
Assessing the pros and cons of change   61
Negotiating and agreeing the introduction of change   62
Implementing and evaluating changes   63

Quality Assurance   65

Assuring quality   66

Time Management   67

Managing your time   68

Operational Management

Meeting Customer Needs

This section is about maintaining an effective operation to meet customer needs.

The checklists will help you to:

- be clear about the needs of your customers
- ensure suppliers provide value for money
- maintain a safe and efficient working environment
- design your operational systems to meet customer specifications
- solve problems for customers when things go wrong.

The process of *Meeting Customer Needs* looks like this:

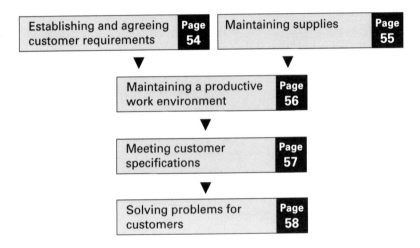

Managing the Operation

Establishing and agreeing customer requirements

1. **Research your customers' needs** - use formal and informal techniques to identify the services or products your customers, or potential customers, need.

2. **Design your services or products to meet your customers' needs** - and ensure your services and products meet legal and organisational requirements and resource constraints.

3. **Describe your services or products clearly** - explain your services or products to customers, think about the person you are talking to, and make sure you communicate in a manner and at a pace which is appropriate.

4. **Encourage customers to discuss their requirements** - invite them to seek clarification wherever appropriate and tell you how well you are meeting their needs.

5. **Communicate frequently with customers** - develop a relationship of trust and goodwill, and keep them informed about any changes which affect them.

6. **Ensure agreements meet legal and organisational requirements** - consult specialists if you are in doubt.

7. **Negotiate effectively** - use your experience of past negotiations to ensure the success of future negotiations.

8. **Optimise agreements** - create a 'win-win' situation, where you achieve your objectives whilst meeting customer needs.

9. **Draw up detailed specifications** - ensure that specifications of customised services or products contain all the relevant information to allow customer requirements to be met.

10. **Keep accurate records** - include all relevant information about customer agreements and implementation plans.

11. **Design customer-focused operations** - organise your operations to provide the most efficient service to your customers.

12. **Develop helpful staff** - encourage your staff to put the customers first and to take personal responsibility for meeting customer needs.

Managing the Operation

Maintaining supplies

1. **Identify the supplies you need** - check they are sufficient to meet customer requirements.

2. **Identify and develop suitable sources of supply** - make sure your suppliers can provide you with the materials you need for your product and services; always have alternative suppliers available for contingencies, if possible.

3. **Select suppliers objectively** - apply fair criteria in choosing your suppliers.

4. **Review your suppliers regularly** - check they continue to offer best value for money and quality of service.

5. **Keep accurate records of suppliers and supplies** - keep a complete list of suppliers' details and monitor levels of supplies regularly.

6. **Watch market and economic trends which may affect supplies** - keep an eye on factors such as raw materials cost/availability, competitor activity or changes to legislation which may affect the price or availability of supplies.

7. **Take action where there are likely to be problems or opportunities with supplies** - where your information suggests changes to supplies which may give you problems or opportunities, take, or recommend, appropriate action to turn the situation to your advantage.

8. **Keep complete and accurate records of negotiations and agreements with suppliers** - and pass this information on to appropriate people as soon as possible.

9. **Maintain goodwill** - throughout your negotiations with suppliers, make sure you retain their goodwill, and find mutually acceptable ways of settling any disputes.

Managing the Operation

Maintaining a productive work environment

1. **Ensure the environment is as conducive to work as possible** - involve your staff in assessing the work environment to see if there are different ways it could be arranged to improve productivity.

2. **Ensure that conditions satisfy legal and organisational requirements** - check the relevant legislation and your internal guidelines, and make sure you have a safe work environment.

3. **Cater for special needs** - provide for any special needs of employees or potential employees to ensure they can work productively.

4. **Make sure equipment is properly maintained and used only by competent personnel** - regularly check all equipment in your area to see that it is properly maintained and that relevant staff have been trained to use it.

5. **Ensure you have a sufficient supply of resources** - plan what materials, equipment and resources you require to keep your operation running smoothly.

6. **Where you do not have sufficient resources, refer to the appropriate people** - let them know immediately if you are likely to run out of anything.

7. **Pass on recommendations for improving conditions** - where you identify opportunities for improving working conditions, let the appropriate people know right away, so the organisation can benefit as soon as possible.

8. **Report accidents and incidents promptly and accurately** - check that you, and your staff, are fully aware of the accident and hazard procedures and that they are followed at all times.

9. **Keep accurate records** - make sure your department's maintenance and health and safety records are accurate, legible and up-to-date.

Meeting customer specifications

1. **Check that specifications are clear, complete and accurate** - where there is any omission or ambiguity, get clarification from your customer.

2. **Draw up plans and schedules to meet these specifications** - allow for contingencies in these plans.

3. **Brief all relevant people** - make sure they understand how the specifications, plans and schedules affect them.

4. **Monitor operations** - monitor what is happening and take appropriate action to ensure specifications are met.

5. **Make best use of resources** - use your human, capital and financial resources efficiently to meet the specifications.

6. **Encourage staff to take responsibility for meeting customer requirements** - involve staff in finding the best way to meet specifications and gain their commitment.

7. **Give staff feedback** - tell them how well they are doing in meeting customer requirements.

8. **Get feedback from customers** - use this feedback to improve future operations.

9. **Minimise disruptions to operations** - take appropriate action to reduce any factors which may disrupt operations.

10. **Take corrective action** - implement any changes without delay and inform relevant staff, colleagues and customers about these.

11. **Monitor corrective action** - make sure that changes are working, and use this experience to improve future operations.

12. **Keep complete and accurate records of operations** - keep records of activities and how well you met customer specifications and make these records available to appropriate people.

Managing the Operation

Solving problems for customers

1. **Design systems to anticipate and avoid problems for customers** - design all your procedures to meet customer needs.

2. **Advise customers about your policies and procedures for solving their problems** - use appropriate media to publish your policies and procedures and alternative sources of assistance to which customers may refer.

3. **Identify and acknowledge the customer's perception of the problem** - where problems do occur, listen carefully in order to understand and acknowledge the customer's view of the problem.

4. **Gather all information relevant to the customer's problem** - refer to records and other people involved in order to get a full picture of the problem.

5. **Summarise the customer's problem** - summarise their perceptions and all other relevant information and check that the customer agrees with your summary of the problem.

6. **Keep the customer informed** - tell the customer how you plan to resolve the problem, how long it will take and give the customer progress reports where appropriate.

7. **Refer to organisational procedures** - examine and interpret procedures for handling customer complaints to identify a solution.

8. **Seek advice from colleagues or senior managers** - where organisational procedures do not offer a satisfactory solution ask colleagues for help in identifying alternative solutions.

9. **Implement the solution promptly** - once the solution has been identified, take prompt action to solve the customer's problem and inform the customer of the action taken.

10. **Monitor the delivery of the solution** - and make appropriate modifications to resolve any problems arising.

11. **Check customer's satisfaction** - where appropriate, check that the problem has been solved to the customer's satisfaction.

12. **Develop new procedures** - review the process and where policies or procedures do not offer a satisfactory solution, revise or develop new policies or procedures to avoid or address similar situations.

Managing Change

This section is about identifying, implementing and evaluating improvements.

The checklists will help you to:

- always be looking for areas where improvements can be made
- assess the benefits against any problems caused by the changes
- consult with all concerned to get them to agree to the changes
- implement your plans for change
- evaluate whether improvements have been achieved.

The process of *Managing Change* looks like this:

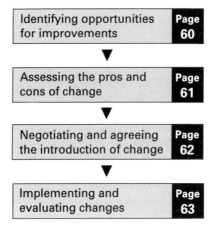

Identifying opportunities for improvements	Page 60
Assessing the pros and cons of change	Page 61
Negotiating and agreeing the introduction of change	Page 62
Implementing and evaluating changes	Page 63

Identifying opportunities for improvements

1. **Keep up to date with developments in your sector** - make sure you get relevant, valid, reliable information from various sources on developments in materials, equipment, technology and processes.

2. **Consider the importance of these developments to your organisation** - carry out a regular review of developments and analyse their significance to your organisation.

3. **Pass information on developments to the appropriate people** - if you think it is important, make sure your colleagues, staff and senior managers are aware of its significance.

4. **Identify opportunities for improvements** - use information on developments to identify opportunities for growth, improvements in procedures or improvements in quality.

5. **Monitor and evaluate your operations continuously** - always look for areas where improvements can be made and take appropriate action.

6. **Identify any obstacles to change** - take appropriate measures to alleviate any problems which may prevent improvements being made.

7. **Learn from your experience** - use your experience of previous improvements to help identify new ones.

Assessing the pros and cons of change

1. **Get complete and accurate information** - make sure you have sufficient, reliable information on both current and proposed services, products and systems to allow you to make a reliable assessment.

2. **Compare the advantages and disadvantages** - use qualitative and quantitative techniques to assess the pros and cons of current and proposed services, products and systems.

3. **Assess the implications of introducing changes** - changes may affect cashflow, working practices, staff morale, supply and distribution networks and customer loyalty; anticipate and assess the likely effect of changes.

4. **Take into account previous assessments of introducing change** - look at how realistic previous assessments turned out to be and use these to modify your current assessment.

5. **Present your recommendations to the appropriate people** - make your recommendations to senior managers or specialists in a way which helps them make a decision and in time to allow the decision to be put into effect.

6. **Amend your recommendations in the light of responses** - make appropriate alterations to your recommendations on the basis of the responses you get from senior managers and specialists.

Managing the Operation

Negotiating and agreeing the introduction of change

1. **Present information on projected change to the appropriate people** - let staff, colleagues, senior managers and others know about the changes at the earliest possible time, and in sufficient detail, to allow them to evaluate its impact on their area of responsibility.

2. **Conduct negotiations in a spirit of goodwill** - make sure you retain the support of others and find mutually acceptable ways of settling any disputes.

3. **Make compromises where appropriate** - it may be necessary to make compromises to accommodate other priorities, but make sure these compromises are consistent with your organisation's strategy, objectives and practices.

4. **Reach an agreement in line with your organisation's strategy** - and include detailed implementation plans.

5. **Keep records of negotiations and agreements** - make sure your records are complete and accurate and that they are available for others to refer to if necessary.

6. **Where you could not secure the changes you anticipated, tell your staff in a positive manner** - sometimes you are disappointed in not being able to obtain the changes you wanted for your team due to other organisational priorities; explain to your staff the reasons for this in a positive way.

7. **Encourage all relevant people to understand and participate in the changes** - communicate the changes and their effects to people, and gain their support.

Managing the Operation

Implementing and evaluating changes

1. **Present details of implementation plans to all concerned** - make sure that you brief everyone involved, or affected by, the changes on their role in the changes and the possible impact on their area.

2. **Encourage people to seek clarification** - check on their understanding of their role and encourage them to ask questions.

3. **Use resources in the most effective way** - plan carefully so that you meet the new requirements as cost-effectively as possible.

4. **Monitor the changes** - check to see that the changes have been implemented according to plan and that they result in the improvements anticipated.

5. **Evaluate the benefits of the changes** - compare the new way of working with the old; are the benefits as expected?

6. **Modify implementation plans and activities in the light of experience** - you may need to modify the way you implement changes to cope with unforeseen problems.

7. **Review the change process** - review the whole process of identifying, assessing, negotiating, agreeing, implementing and evaluating change, note ways of doing it better next time and make appropriate recommendations to senior managers, colleagues and specialists.

Managing the Operation

Quality Assurance

This section is about developing systems to ensure that you meet your customers needs on time, every time.

The checklist will help you to:

- be clear about your customers' needs
- involve staff and other colleagues in developing quality assurance systems
- monitor and publicise the benefits of quality assurance systems.

This section links closely with the sections on *Meeting Customer Needs* and *Managing Change*. It has just one checklist:

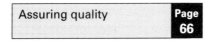

| Assuring quality | Page 66 |

Refer also to the checklist on *Assuring Quality* (pages 33-45) in the section on Quality Management.

Quality Assurance

Assuring quality

1. **Be clear about your customers' expectations and requirements** - quality is about fulfilling your customers' expectations on time, every time.

2. **Make recommendations for quality assurance systems to meet customers' expectations** - make sure your systems are in place to meet customer requirements, not to satisfy a bureaucratic whim.

3. **Encourage staff to help develop quality assurance systems** - consult the staff who are most involved with the operation to get their ideas and gain their commitment to following the quality assurance system.

4. **Present details of the quality assurance system, or modifications to it, to all those concerned** - make sure that you brief everyone involved or affected by the quality assurance system on their role or the possible impact on their area.

5. **Encourage people to seek clarification** - check on their understanding of their role and encourage them to ask questions.

6. **Make the best use of resources** - make sure your quality assurance system does not duplicate or add unnecessarily to the workload, but makes best use of existing procedures and activities.

7. **Publicise the benefits and results of quality assurance** - enhance employee commitment and customer satisfaction by making sure they are aware of the benefits that the quality assurance system is delivering.

8. **Monitor your quality assurance systems** - check whether they continue to deliver customer satisfaction and make any modifications required.

Time Management

This section is about making the most efficient use of your time.

The checklist will help you to:

- be clear about your objectives and your priorities
- plan your time and allow for contingencies
- delegate work where appropriate
- be decisive.

This section will help you with all other aspects of management. It has just one checklist:

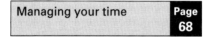

| Managing your time | Page 68 |

Managing your time

1. **Be clear about your objectives** - be clear about what you have to achieve, by when and what the priorities are.

2. **Identify what needs to be done to achieve these objectives** - identify what you, and others, need to do to achieve your objectives and estimate how long each activity will take.

3. **Plan your time** - plan these activities into your time on an annual, monthly, weekly and daily basis to ensure objectives are achieved on time; include time for evaluation.

4. **Delegate** - review your activities and, where possible, delegate those activities which could be done equally well by one of your staff, with training and guidance where appropriate.

5. **Handle paper once only** - when dealing with paper, decide immediately to respond, refer, file or destroy.

6. **Take decisions** - when faced with a choice, either make your choice or decide what further information you need to be able to make an informed choice.

7. **Control interruptions** - make it clear when you welcome consultation with others, and when you require uninterrupted time to complete an activity.

Managing People

Management is about meeting customer requirements with and through people. It involves:

Personnel Planning — 71

Planning human resource requirements — 72
Drawing up job specifications — 73
Assessing and selecting staff — 74
Making staff redundant — 75

Developing Teams and Individuals — 77

Developing teams — 78
Developing individuals — 79
Developing yourself — 80
Coaching — 81
Mentoring — 82
Evaluating and improving training and development — 83

Managing Teams and Individuals — 85

Planning work — 86
Allocating work — 87
Setting objectives — 88
Giving feedback — 89

Working Relationships — 91

Building a relationship with your manager — 92
Building relationships with staff — 93
Building relationships with colleagues — 94
Minimising conflict — 95

Managing Problems with Staff — 97

Counselling — 98
Implementing grievance and disciplinary procedures — 99
Firing staff — 100

Equal Opportunities — 101

Promoting equal opportunities — 102
Encouraging diversity and fair working practices — 103

Operational Management

Personnel Planning

This section is about making sure you have the right people to do the jobs.

The checklists will help you to:

- be clear about the people you need to meet your organisational objectives
- specify the skills, qualities and attributes you are looking for in staff
- assess candidates against specific criteria and select those most appropriate
- make redundant those staff who are no longer required.

The process for *Personnel Planning* looks like this

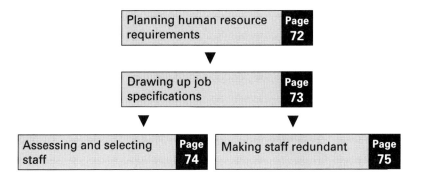

Planning human resource requirements — Page 72

Drawing up job specifications — Page 73

Assessing and selecting staff — Page 74

Making staff redundant — Page 75

Managing People

Planning human resource requirements

1. **Identify the optimum human resources required to achieve objectives** - you will need people to help you achieve the objectives of your organisation, department, team or project; identify the number and type of staff needed to provide you with the best support at the most reasonable cost.

2. **Base your plans on current, valid and reliable information** - check your information is sound and up-to-date.

3. **Support your plans with appropriate calculations** - your estimates of the human resource required will need to be supported by calculations of the time required to complete tasks and the associated personnel costs, including training and development, and provision for special needs.

4. **Identify the skills and personal qualities required of the team and individuals** - look for a balance of strengths within the team.

5. **Be clear about organisational constraints** - specify where financial considerations, organisational policy or legal constraints affect your plans.

6. **Consult with colleagues and staff** - take into account the views of your colleagues, specialists and your staff on how best to meet your future human resource requirements.

7. **Present your plans on time and with the appropriate level of detail** - make sure your plans are accurate, contain sufficient detail for a decision to be made and are presented in time for you to take the necessary action.

Drawing up job specifications

1. **Be clear about the job role** - clearly state the purpose of the job and how it relates to organisational objectives and the team.

2. **Specify the job in sufficient detail** - think carefully about the job title, reporting relationships, key objectives and responsibilities and the terms and conditions of service.

3. **Specify the type of person required** - be clear about the knowledge, competences and qualities they will need.

4. **Consult with colleagues and staff** - take into account the views of your colleagues, specialists and your staff on the definition of the job and the skills, knowledge and qualities required.

5. **Check that the specification is clear, concise and complies with legal and organisational requirements** - consult with specialists if you are in doubt.

6. **Agree the specification with appropriate people** - check and agree the specification with colleagues, specialists and your staff before taking any action to recruit, transfer or change a person's job.

7. **Regularly review job specifications** - keep specifications under review to ensure that they still describe the job and meet the organisation's needs.

Managing People

Assessing and selecting staff

1. **Check your organisation's procedures and legal requirements** - make sure that your process for assessing and selecting staff complies with your organisation's procedures and the law.

2. **Obtain, or draw up, criteria against which to judge candidates** - have clear, measurable criteria.

3. **Seek advice if you are not sure about any of the selection criteria** - consult with specialists if you are in doubt.

4. **Get sufficient information from candidates to be able to make a decision** - use a variety of appropriate assessment techniques, cv's, application forms, interviews, tests, references etc, to ensure you get all relevant information.

5. **Judge the information obtained against specified selection criteria** - you should be able to defend your decision to accept or reject a candidate by how well the candidates meet the selection criteria; do not let irrelevant factors affect your decision.

6. **Be fair and consistent** - correct any deviations from agreed procedures before you make your selection.

7. **Maintain confidentiality** - tell only authorised people of your selection recommendations.

8. **Keep clear, accurate and complete records** - you may need to refer back to them.

9. **Keep candidates informed** - tell candidates promptly and accurately of decisions following each stage of the selection process.

10. **Check that your choice is justifiable** - make sure you have selected the most suitable candidate from the evidence obtained and the process used; if in doubt, consult colleagues or specialists.

11. **Review the process and make appropriate recommendations for improvement** - consider every aspect of the process and make any recommendations for improving it, so that you and your colleagues can do better next time.

Making staff redundant

1. **Keep staff informed about current procedures** - ensure that staff are aware of your organisation's policy and any redundancy procedures, including appeals procedure.
2. **Avoid redundancies where possible** - accurate personnel planning will minimise the need for redundancies, but where these are inevitable explore alternatives such as early retirement or part-time working.
3. **Consult with staff** - consult with both individual staff and their representatives over the redundancy plan. Consultation will improve co-operation and may result in alternative, more acceptable approaches being adopted.
4. **Agree clear and fair selection criteria** - agree selection criteria which are unambiguous, can be clearly applied, are fair and comply with legal and organisational requirements.
5. **Apply selection criteria fairly and consistently** - consult with specialists if you are in doubt.
6. **Prepare to break the news** - rehearse what you will say to staff who will be made redundant, including responses to likely questions, and enlist the support of colleagues or specialists, as advised.
7. **Break the news quickly and compassionately** - tell staff quickly, clearly, confidentially and compassionately that they will be made redundant and what help is available to them.
8. **Offer alternative work** - where there are suitable jobs available, offer these alternatives with details of terms and conditions.
9. **Offer counselling** - offer staff appropriate counselling, resources, training and time off work to help them find another job and cope with the personal and practical implications of redundancy.
10. **Seek advice** - seek advice from colleagues and specialists, on all aspects of making staff redundant in order to ensure you comply with legal and organisational requirements.
11. **Keep staff and colleagues informed** - tell staff and colleagues about the redundancies and the reasons, without breaching confidentiality.
12. **Recommend any changes to policy or procedures** - tell the appropriate people of ways in which your organisation's policy or procedures could be improved.

Managing People

Developing Teams and Individuals

This section is about making sure your team has the skills to do their jobs.

The checklists will help you to:
- develop a balanced team with all the skills needed
- help individuals identify and develop the skills they need
- develop the skills you need for your job
- coach individuals to develop new skills
- be an adviser or mentor to individuals to help them develop
- evaluate and improve the training and development processes.

The process for *Developing Teams and Individuals* looks like this:

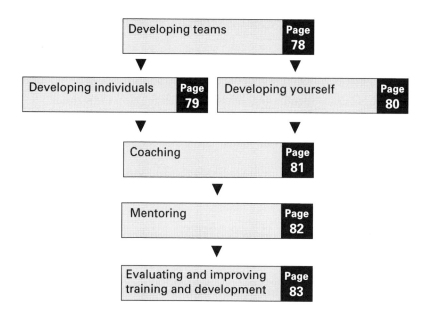

ıg teams

all team members in evaluating the team's
ıment needs - get them involved in identifying their own
strengths and weaknesses.

2. **Assess the team's strengths and weaknesses** - looking at each
   individual and at the team as a whole, assess and acknowledge the
   team's strengths and weaknesses to carry out current and future
   work.

3. **Consult with all team members on how to meet development
   needs** - gain the team's commitment by involving them in
   planning how to meet development needs.

4. **Be clear about the objectives of development plans** - your
   objectives should be clear, relevant and realistic for individuals and
   the team as a whole.

5. **Optimise the use of resources** - when planning development
   activities, use available resources effectively.

6. **Minimise unproductive friction** - be clear about individuals'
   responsibilities in the team to minimise risk of bad feeling.

7. **Regularly review your plans** - discuss and agree improvements to
   development plans with team members, other colleagues and
   specialists at appropriate intervals.

Developing individuals

1. **Involve individuals in identifying their own developm**
   needs - get them to identify their own strengths and weakn

2. **Discuss development needs and plans with individuals** - gain
   their commitment by involving individuals in planning how to
   meet their development needs.

3. **Be clear about the objectives of development plans** - your
   objectives should be clear, relevant and realistic for the individual.

4. **Balance business needs with individual aspirations** - plans
   should help individuals to develop the skills they need to do their
   current job and meet future job requirements and career
   aspirations.

5. **Optimise the use of resources** - when planning development
   activities, use available resources effectively.

6. **Regularly review your plans** - regularly discuss and agree
   improvements to development plans with individuals, other
   colleagues and specialists.

Managing People

Developing yourself

1. **Take responsibility for developing yourself** - ensure you develop the skills you need to achieve your objectives.

2. **Identify your own strengths and weaknesses** - measure your current skills as a manager against appropriate standards and by getting feedback from your line manager, colleagues and staff.

3. **Set yourself clear development objectives** - make your objectives achievable, realistic and challenging.

4. **Consider the needs of the organisation** - include objectives to develop as a team member.

5. **Allow sufficient time and resources** - allocate sufficient time and appropriate resources to achieve your development objectives.

6. **Regularly review progress and performance** - check your progress against your objectives with your line manager and specialists at regular intervals and revise your plan as appropriate.

7. **Compare feedback with your own perceptions of your performance** - compare feedback from your line manager, colleagues, staff and others with how well you think you are doing; and improve your future performance as a result.

Coaching

1. **Identify the individual's development needs** - use appropriate methods to assess the needs of the person you are coaching.

2. **Agree learning objectives** - discuss and agree with the individual the learning objectives to be achieved.

3. **Take account of the individual** - design your coaching to match the individual's learning preferences, and deliver the coaching in a manner and at a pace appropriate to the learner.

4. **Analyse the components of skills** - make sure you understand the different components of the skill and convey these in the sequence in which they need to be learnt.

5. **Identify inhibiting factors** - clearly identify and discuss with learners any factors which are inhibiting their learning.

6. **Check learners' progress** - check regularly on progress and modify coaching as appropriate.

7. **Give feedback** - provide timely feedback to learners on the process of learning and on their progress towards learning objectives in a positive and encouraging manner.

8. **Receive feedback** - ask learners how they feel about the process of learning and their speed of progress and modify coaching as appropriate.

Managing People

e individual's learning objectives - discuss and
: learning objectives to be achieved with individual
heir line managers and others involved.

2. **Agree the support mentees require** - specify and agree the roles, responsibilities and resources needed to help mentees achieve their learning objectives.

3. **Identify and overcome any difficulties in obtaining this support** - identify likely difficulties in obtaining the necessary people and resources and agree ways of overcoming these difficulties.

4. **Develop effective working relationships** - both with mentees and with others who can provide support.

5. **Provide guidance** - provide accurate, timely and appropriate advice and guidance on learning methods and opportunities, and on other sources of information and advice.

6. **Encourage independent decision-making** - provide guidance in a way which encourages mentees to take responsibility for their own development and enables them to make informed decisions.

7. **Facilitate learning and assessment opportunities** - identify and facilitate opportunities for mentees to develop, practice, apply and assess new skills, knowledge and experience in a structured way.

8. **Provide on-going support** - within the agreed role, provide mentees with support for their learning, development and assessment, as required.

9. **Give feedback** - provide timely feedback to mentees on their progress towards learning objectives in a positive and encouraging manner.

10. **Review the mentoring process** - at appropriate intervals, discuss the mentoring process and your relationship with mentees and modify as appropriate.

Developing Teams and Individuals

Evaluating and improving training and development

1. **Identify clearly the training and development objectives** - be clear what the objectives are and how to measure whether they have been achieved.

2. **Debrief the learners** - discuss with individuals and teams involved in training and development how useful it was, how satisfied they were with its delivery and how well it will apply to their work.

3. **Find suitable alternatives where training and development did not meet the needs** - discuss and agree with the individuals and teams concerned alternative training and development which may be more appropriate.

4. **Modify team and individual training and development plans** - where plans were unrealistic, discuss and agree modified plans with the teams and individuals concerned.

5. **Check whether objectives have been achieved** - apply the agreed measures to see to what extent objectives have been achieved.

6. **Pass on your experience** - discuss the strengths and weaknesses of the training and development processes used with specialists, your line manager and colleagues so they can gain from your experience.

7. **Benefit from your experience** - use your experience of training and development processes to help you identify more appropriate training and development in the future.

Managing Teams and Individuals

This section is about making sure your team get the job done.

The checklists will help you to:

- plan the work to meet your objectives
- allocate work amongst the team
- set clear objectives for each member of the team
- evaluate performance and provide feedback to staff.

The process for *Managing Teams and Individuals* looks like this:

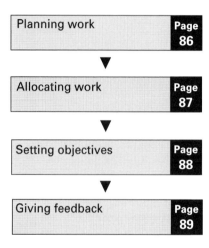

| Planning work | Page 86 |

▼

| Allocating work | Page 87 |

▼

| Setting objectives | Page 88 |

▼

| Giving feedback | Page 89 |

Planning work

1. **Plan work in order to meet organisational objectives** - make sure your plans are consistent with team and organisational objectives.

2. **Assess the degree of direction required by each member of staff** - inexperienced or less confident staff may need far more direction and help in planning their work than more experienced and self-assured colleagues.

3. **Encourage individuals to contribute to planning work activities and methods** - the staff who will be carrying out the work are likely to have sound ideas as to the most efficient ways of doing it.

4. **Include staff suggestions on working methods, resources and time required** - this will help to ensure their commitment to the work.

5. **Select work methods and activities which meet both operational and developmental objectives** - choose work methods and activities which balance management priorities, organisational objectives, legal requirements and opportunities for individual development.

6. **Select cost-effective work methods** - choose work methods which make the best use of available material, capital and people.

7. **Seek advice where legal requirements and organisational/developmental objectives conflict** - consult with your line manager, specialists or external advisers.

Allocating work

1. **Allocate work according to availability of resources and skills of staff** - optimise the resources and the skills of the staff available to meet organisational objectives.

2. **Clearly define team and individual responsibilities and limits of authority** - make sure staff understand their own responsibilities and limits of authority, and those with whom they work closely, in order to avoid possible conflict, duplication or omission of important responsibilities.

3. **Provide learning and developmental opportunities for staff within the work allocated** - take opportunities to develop new skills which staff will need in the future.

4. **Brief staff on their work in a manner and at a level and pace which is appropriate** - inexperienced or less confident staff may need a more detailed briefing on their responsibilities and work than their more experienced and self-assured colleagues.

5. **Encourage staff to seek clarification** - check on their understanding and give them opportunities to ask questions.

6. **Provide access to people who can help them meet their objectives** - staff may need access to colleagues, managers, specialists and external advisers to help them meet their work and developmental objectives.

7. **Provide the right level of supervision** - some staff will require much closer supervision than others.

8. **Ensure that work allocations are realistic** - carefully calculate the time, cost and criticality of the work to ensure appropriate resources have been allocated.

9. **Reallocate work where appropriate** - if the way work was allocated proves to be unrealistic, or organisational demands change, reallocate work whilst minimising any detrimental impact on time or cost.

10. **Benefit from your experience** - evaluate how well you have allocated work in order to improve your performance in the future.

Managing People

Setting objectives

1. **Involve staff in setting objectives** - ask staff to be proactive in identifying what their objectives should be.

2. **Set clear objectives** - agree SMART objectives with your staff which are:
Specific	- be precise about what must be achieved
Measurable	- how will you know if it has been achieved?
Agreed	- by you, the member of staff and the team
Realistic	- objectives have to be achievable
Time-bound	- to be completed by a specified time.

3. **Explain objectives clearly** - when explaining objectives, think about the person you are talking to, and make sure you communicate with them in a manner and at a pace which is appropriate.

4. **Encourage staff to seek clarification** - check on their understanding and give them opportunities to ask questions.

5. **Update objectives regularly** - review objectives as often as appropriate in the light of changes to individual and team workloads and organisational priorities.

6. **Check that objectives have been achieved** - as part of the objective-setting process, agree the date when you will review with your staff whether the objectives have been achieved.

7. **Provide feedback** - both formally and informally which includes constructive suggestions and encouragement for improving future performance.

Giving feedback

1. **Seek opportunities to provide feedback to teams and individuals on their performance** - feedback helps people to understand if they are doing a good job or if there are areas in which they can improve. Feedback can be given formally or informally, orally or in writing.

2. **Choose an appropriate time and place to give the feedback** - feedback is more useful and relevant if provided quickly. Sometimes it is appropriate to give feedback publicly, but often a quiet word with a member of staff is what is required.

3. **Recognise good performance and achievement** - take opportunities to congratulate staff on their successes.

4. **Provide constructive suggestions and encouragement for improving future performance** - when staff are not performing well, tell them, and advise them how they can improve.

5. **Encourage staff to contribute to their own assessment** - ask open-ended questions about how they view their performance and invite them to be specific.

6. **Provide feedback in sufficient detail and in a manner and at a level and pace which is appropriate to the staff concerned** - some staff may readily understand your feedback on their performance, with others it may be necessary to be very specific about their performance and any improvements required.

7. **Encourage staff to seek clarification** - check their understanding and give them the opportunity to ask questions.

8. **Encourage staff to make suggestions on how systems/ procedures could be improved** - their performance may be greatly enhanced by changes to procedures and working practices.

9. **Record details of any action agreed** - make a note of actions agreed to maintain or improve their performance or change procedures, and inform the appropriate people.

10. **Review performance** - check back at an appropriate point to see whether performance has improved or been maintained.

Managing People

Working Relationships

This section is about building effective working relationships with all those you work with.

The checklists will help you to:

- take time to build effective working relationships
- consult with colleagues and keep them informed
- be honest and open with people
- provide support and keep your promises
- take steps to minimise any possible conflicts.

The process of building effective *Working Relationships* looks like this

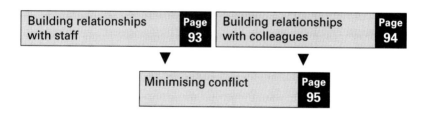

Building a relationship with your manager

1. **Keep your manager informed** - provide an appropriate level of detail about activities, progress, results and achievements.

2. **Provide information about emerging threats and opportunities** - let your manager know about possible threats and opportunities clearly, accurately and with the appropriate level of urgency.

3. **Seek information and advice** - ask your manager for information and advice on policy and ways of working whenever appropriate.

4. **Present clear proposals for action** - present proposals at the appropriate time and with the right level of detail. Your manager will require more detail the greater the degree of change, expenditure and risk involved in your proposal.

5. **Identify the reasons why a proposal has been rejected** - try to find out clearly what the reasons are and, if appropriate, put forward alternative proposals.

6. **Make efforts to maintain a good relationship with your manager** - even if you do have disagreements, try to prevent these damaging your relationship.

7. **Meet your objectives** - always try to fulfil the objectives agreed with your manager in full; where circumstances prevent you from meeting objectives, inform your manager at the earliest possible time.

8. **Support your manager** - give your manager your backing, especially in situations which involve people outside your team.

9. **Be open and direct** - discuss any concerns about the relationship with your manager directly with him or her.

Building relationships with staff

1. **Take time to build honest and constructive relationships with staff** - get to know your staff and allow them to get to know you.

2. **Keep staff informed** - provide them with relevant information on organisational policy and strategy, progress, emerging threats and opportunities.

3. **Consult staff about proposed activities** - give them the opportunity to state their views so they can be taken into account.

4. **Encourage staff to offer their ideas and views** - use open questions to get their contributions.

5. **Give recognition for their ideas and views** - thank them and show the value you place on their ideas.

6. **Give clear reasons where ideas are not taken up** - where it is not possible to take up a good idea, acknowledge the value of the idea and explain why it is not possible to adopt it.

7. **Encourage staff to seek clarification** - check their understanding and give them the opportunity to ask questions.

8. **Keep your promises** - when you make promises and undertakings to staff, make sure they are realistic and that you honour them.

9. **Support your staff** - give staff your backing especially in situations which involve people outside your team.

10. **Be open and direct** - discuss concerns about the quality of work directly with the member of staff concerned.

Managing People

Building relationships with colleagues

1. **Take time to build honest and constructive relationships with colleagues** - get to know your colleagues and allow them to get to know you.

2. **Encourage open, honest and friendly behaviour** - ask open questions to get their opinions.

3. **Share information and opinions with colleagues** - stop and think who could benefit from any information or idea you have.

4. **Offer help and advice with sensitivity** - you can often help a colleague or provide advice on a difficult problem.

5. **Deal courteously with colleagues when you have differences of opinion** - you will not always agree with colleagues; discuss these different views respectfully and try to understand them.

6. **Resolve conflicts amicably** - always maintain mutual respect.

7. **Keep your promises** - when you make promises to colleagues, make sure they are realistic and that you honour them.

Minimising conflict

1. **Explain to staff the standards of work and behaviour you expect** - some staff will readily appreciate the standards you and your organisation require; others may require a fuller and more detailed explanation.

2. **Clearly allocate work and responsibilities** - you can greatly reduce the potential for conflict by making sure your staff are clear about the responsibilities of each member of the team.

3. **Encourage staff to discuss problems which affect their work** - make it clear that you are available to help resolve these problems.

4. **Quickly identify potential or actual conflicts between staff** - when conflicts appear, or are likely, involve the relevant staff in identifying the nature and cause of the conflict early on.

5. **Take prompt action to resolve conflicts** - do not let the conflict fester, but take decisive action to deal with it.

6. **Ensure solutions satisfy legal and organisational requirements** - check that you are not infringing any legislation or procedures and that your solution helps meet organisational objectives.

7. **Keep accurate and complete records of the conflict** - particularly where the conflict is serious, keep notes of what happened and what was agreed, in case there is any comeback.

8. **Monitor the situation** - keep an eye on the situation to ensure that the conflict does not reappear.

9. **Learn from your experience** - use the experience to help you, and your staff, avoid or quickly resolve conflicts in the future.

Managing People

Managing Problems with Staff

This section is about ensuring the best outcome when you have problems with staff.

The checklists will help you to:

- counsel staff when personal matters are affecting their work
- action grievance and disciplinary procedures
- dismiss staff, where this is the most appropriate option.

This section covers:

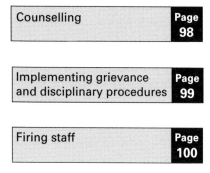

| Counselling | Page 98 |

| Implementing grievance and disciplinary procedures | Page 99 |

| Firing staff | Page 100 |

Managing People

selling

1. ntify the need for counselling quickly - be alert to the need to counsel staff; changes in mood, a fall-off in performance, stress symptoms, or a word from a colleague may indicate the need to counsel staff.

2. **Choose an appropriate time and place** - counselling on personal matters affecting an individual's work needs to take place in a private place and at a time which allows for full discussion without interruptions.

3. **Follow your organisation's guidelines or personnel policies** - if your organisation has specified personnel policies, check to make sure you follow these.

4. **Encourage the individual to discuss the situation fully** - help the individual to understand the situation and all the factors which affect it.

5. **Encourage the individual to take responsibility for their own decisions and actions** - remember you are helping them to solve a problem, you are not solving it for them.

6. **Recommend an appropriate counselling service where appropriate** - when you do not have the skills or knowledge to help the individual, recommend they see a specialist in your organisation or an external counselling service, doctor etc.

7. **Monitor the situation** - keep an eye on the situation and offer further counselling sessions if these are necessary.

Managing People

Implementing grievance and disciplinary procedures

1. **Keep staff informed about current procedures** - make sure they have up-to-date copies of your organisation's grievance and disciplinary procedures and remind them of these from time to time.

2. **Action grievance and disciplinary procedures with minimum delay** - act promptly to prevent the situation getting out of hand and causing damage to the organisation or the staff concerned.

3. **Act in accordance with legal and organisational requirements** - check, with a specialist if necessary, both the legal situation and your organisation's procedures.

4. **Ask for advice** - where appropriate, confidentially ask a specialist, your line manager or colleagues for advice on how to deal effectively with these difficult situations, especially where legal and organisational requirements conflict.

5. **Involve a third party** - where appropriate, ask a third party - specialist, line manager or colleague - to become involved to ensure you implement the procedures fairly and impartially.

6. **Be, and be seen to be, impartial** - get all the facts of the case before you and make decisions which are objective and can be shown to be free of personal bias.

7. **Keep accurate and complete records** - make detailed notes of the whole proceedings and, where appropriate, copy these to the member(s) of staff concerned and specialists.

8. **Monitor the situation** - keep an eye on the situation to ensure that the problems which led to the implementation of grievance or disciplinary procedures do not reappear.

9. **Learn from your experience** - use the experience to help you, and your staff, avoid or quickly resolve the problems in the future.

10. **Recommend any improvements to the procedures** - tell the appropriate people of any ways in which the procedures could be improved.

Managing People

Firing staff

1. **Avoid the need to fire staff wherever possible** - good recruitment and selection, training, development and counselling techniques will minimise the need to fire staff.

2. **Follow disciplinary procedures** - make sure you follow your organisation's disciplinary procedures in detail.

3. **Seek advice** - seek advice from colleagues and specialists, inside or outside your organisation, on all aspects of firing staff in order to ensure you comply with legal and organisational requirements.

4. **Involve a third party** - where appropriate, ask a third party - specialist, line manager or colleague - to become involved to ensure you follow procedures fairly and impartially.

5. **Get the facts** - make sure you get all information relevant to the dismissal. If necessary, suspend the member of staff on full pay until you have all the facts available.

6. **Prepare to break the news** - rehearse what you will say to the member of staff, including responses to likely questions, and enlist the support of colleagues or specialists as appropriate.

7. **Give clear, fair grounds for dismissal** - check that your reasons for dismissing the member of staff are clear and fair grounds for dismissal, and give these both orally and in writing.

8. **Summarily dismiss staff in the case of gross misconduct** - dismiss staff without notice or pay in lieu of notice in the event of gross misconduct. When in doubt, suspend on full pay until you can consult specialists or gather all the facts.

9. **Keep staff and colleagues informed** - tell staff and colleagues about the dismissal and the reasons, without breaching confidentiality.

10. **Review the procedures and reasons for dismissal** - tell the appropriate people of any ways in which the procedures could be improved or future dismissals avoided.

Equal Opportunities

This section is about providing equal working opportunities, encouraging diversity and discouraging unfair discrimination.

The checklists will help you to:

- develop, implement and evaluate your equal opportunities policy and action plan
- encourage staff to use a range of appropriate working styles
- promote fair working practices.

The process of managing *Equal Opportunities* looks like this:

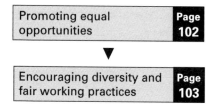

Promoting equal opportunities	Page 102

▼

Encouraging diversity and fair working practices	Page 103

Managing People

Equal Opportunities

Promoting equal opportunities

1. **Contribute to the development of your organisation's equal opportunities policy** - offer your views and recommendations on how the policy should be developed.

2. **Involve staff, colleagues and customers** - encourage them to help develop your equal opportunities action plan, identify areas where opportunities are unfairly restricted and gain their commitment to the plan.

3. **Agree measures** - specify the criteria by which you can assess progress in your action plan.

4. **Collect and analyse information** - find out whether some groups of potential customers are excluded from obtaining your services or products; check whether certain employees, or potential employees, are denied access to development, employment or promotion opportunities.

5. **Identify the strengths of all employees** - especially those from under-represented groups, and identify how these strengths can contribute to your organisation's objectives.

6. **Identify special needs** - identify any special needs of customers, potential customers, employees or potential employees.

7. **Publish your action plan** - including actions to meet special needs and address any imbalances, as well as taking positive action to support under-represented groups.

8. **Communicate action plan to staff** - make sure staff are aware of their responsibilities and duties within the equal opportunities policy and action plan.

9. **Provide training and development opportunities** - provide appropriate training and development to help staff fulfil their duties in the action plan.

10. **Implement your action plan and evaluate your performance** - use agreed measures to monitor your progress against the action plan and modify the plan as appropriate.

Encouraging diversity and fair working practices

1. **Communicate your equal opportunities policy to staff** - make sure staff are aware of the standards of behaviour expected of them and the consequences of unacceptable behaviour.

2. **Encourage a diversity of working styles** - encourage staff to develop a repertoire of appropriate working styles.

3. **Support natural working styles and behaviour** - encourage staff to use their natural and preferred working style and behaviour as long as they are consistent with the achievement of your organisational objectives.

4. **Discourage stereotyping** - discourage staff from imposing stereotypes and styles of working which are inconsistent with individuals' backgrounds.

5. **Discourage rigid approaches** - where particular styles of working are inhibited without good work-related reasons, provide feedback and suggestions to encourage more diverse approaches.

6. **Give feedback and suggestions sensitively** - where the style of working is inhibiting achievement of objectives, give feedback and suggestions to individuals in ways which are sensitive to their racial, social, gender or physical circumstances.

7. **Challenge discriminatory behaviour** - clearly explain the problems this behaviour may cause and the sanctions which will be applied if it continues.

8. **Implement disciplinary procedures** - take prompt action where unfair discriminatory behaviour persists.

9. **Seek guidance and support** - where you are unsure of the effect of your own, a member of your staff's or a colleague's behaviour on another person, seek guidance and support from specialists, inside or outside your organisation.

Managing People

Managing Finance

Managing Finance is about establishing and agreeing budgets for providing services to customers, and ensuring that costs are kept to a minimum. It involves:

Managing Budgets   **107**

    Preparing budgets   108
    Negotiating and agreeing budgets   109
    Monitoring budgets   110

Cost Control   **111**

    Controlling costs   112

Operational Management

Managing Budgets

This section is about making sure projects and operations meet their financial targets.

The checklists will help you to:

* prepare estimates of income and expenditure based on the best information available
* negotiate effectively with those who have to agree the budget
* regularly check on performance against budget and make modifications where appropriate.

The process for *Managing Budgets* looks like this:

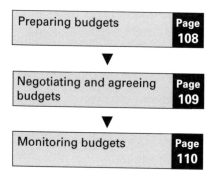

Preparing budgets	**Page 108**
▼	
Negotiating and agreeing budgets	**Page 109**
▼	
Monitoring budgets	**Page 110**

Managing Finance

Managing Budgets

Preparing budgets

1. **Prepare accurate estimates of benefits, income and costs** - base your estimates on valid, reliable information, with historical data and trends where available.

2. **Assess alternative courses of action** - before submitting your budget and recommending expenditure assess the relative benefits and costs of alternative courses of action.

3. **Encourage staff to contribute to the budget** - if staff are involved in the process of drawing up the budget, they will be more committed to achieving the benefits and income and keeping within agreed costs.

4. **Clearly indicate the benefits over time** - be sure to specify what will be the net benefit from the expenditure.

5. **State your assumptions** - make it clear what assumptions you have made and why.

6. **Allow for contingencies** - take into account future changes which may affect the level of income and expenditure.

7. **Check your budgets with others** - where other people have been involved in providing information or making suggestions, check the details with them before submitting your final budget.

8. **Present your budget clearly and concisely** - make use of any forms which your organisation may have developed for presenting budgets.

9. **Be prepared to give a fuller explanation** - have all your information and arguments to hand to counter any challenges to your proposed budget.

10. **Learn from your experience** - compare actual costs and benefits with the budget and use this information to help you improve your budgeting in the future.

Managing Finance

Negotiating and agreeing budgets

1. **Prepare people in advance** - involve your staff, colleagues and those who will be agreeing the budgets in discussing assumptions and drawing up the budgets.

2. **State your assumptions and the contingencies allowed for** - make it clear what assumptions you have made and what contingencies you have anticipated.

3. **Present your budget clearly and concisely** - emphasise the benefits making use of any forms the organisation may have developed for presenting budgets.

4. **Be as accurate as you can in your estimates** - use all the information available to support your calculations.

5. **Allow sufficient time for negotiation** - present your budget sufficiently early to allow you to provide further information if required.

6. **Negotiate with a spirit of good-will** - show that you intend to find a mutually acceptable solution.

7. **Seek clarification where there is uncertainty or disagreement** - ask for guidance and help in finding a mutually acceptable solution.

8. **Publish the budget decisions** - tell all those concerned about the outcomes of budget negotiations promptly, in order to secure their support, co-operation and confidence.

Monitoring budgets

1. **Keep expenditure within agreed limits** - be clear what your budget limits are, make sure you keep within these and check that all expenditure conforms to your organisation's policies and procedures.

2. **Phase expenditure according to a planned time-scale** - make sure you do not overspend your budget in any period, even if you are still within budget for the year, as this will be detrimental to cashflow.

3. **Check actual income and expenditure against budgets** - get accurate information on sales and costs at appropriate intervals.

4. **Report any likely over or underspend against budget** - let the appropriate people know as soon as possible of any potential variance against budget.

5. **Report any likely variance in income against budget** - let the appropriate people know as soon as possible if income is likely to be under or over budget.

6. **Give the reasons for any variances** - analyse the causes for variances in income or expenditure and propose corrective action.

7. **Take prompt corrective action** - take appropriate action where there are actual or potential significant deviations from budget.

8. **Get authority for changes in allocations between budget heads** - where you need to spend more in one budget head and less in another, obtain any necessary authorisation from the appropriate people.

9. **Get approval for changes to budgets** - where you need to change your budget during the accounting period, get appproval from the appropriate people.

Cost Control

This section is about ensuring everybody is continuously looking for ways of controlling or reducing costs.

The checklist will help you to:

- make your team aware how they can help control costs
- keep tight control on expenditure
- take prompt corrective action where expenditure looks like getting out of control.

This section links closely with *Managing Budgets* and *Managing Change*. It has just one checklist:

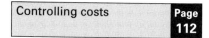

| Controlling costs | Page 112 |

Controlling costs

1. **Make every member of your team aware of how they can help to control costs** - get them to consider areas where costs could be reduced and bring to their attention costs they could help to reduce.

2. **Keep expenditure within agreed budgets** - know what your budget limits are and check that you keep within them.

3. **Where expenditure is outside your responsibility, refer requests promptly to the appropriate people** - many costs are the responsibility of another department; let them know promptly if you need their authorisation for expenditure.

4. **Keep records of expenditure** - keep accurate and complete records available for reference.

5. **Carefully assess information on costs and the use of resources** - regular reviews of costs will help you identify areas where these can be reduced or resources better utilised.

6. **Look for improvements** - make recommendations for efficiency improvements as quickly as possible to the appropriate people.

7. **Take prompt corrective action** - where expenditure is likely to exceed budget, report this immediately to the appropriate people and take action to minimise the effects.

Managing Information

Managing Information is about ensuring prompt access to information in order to make decisions. It involves:

Using Information   **115**

Obtaining and evaluating information   116
Recording and storing information   117
Forecasting trends and developments   118
Presenting information and advice   119

Meetings   **121**

Leading meetings   122
Participating in meetings   123

Operational Management

Using Information

This section is about obtaining, using and presenting information to aid decision-making.

The checklists will help you to:

- identify and obtain the information you need
- record and store information in a way which makes it easy to retrieve
- evaluate the value of information
- use information to forecast future trends and developments
- present information and provide advice to others.

The process of *Using Information* looks like this:

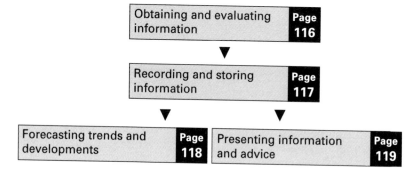

Obtaining and evaluating information

1. **Identify what information you require** - regularly consider the kind of information you are going to need.

2. **Review your sources of information** - regularly review a wide range of sources of information and consider how useful, reliable and cost-effective they are.

3. **Develop your networks** - establish, maintain and develop contacts with people who may be able to provide you with useful information.

4. **Seek out all relevant information** - make sure you have information on all relevant factors affecting current or potential operations.

5. **Try alternative ways of getting information** - if you are having trouble getting information from one source, try a different route in, or an alternative source.

6. **Collect information in time for it to be of use** - make sure information arrives before the deadline.

7. **Present information in a suitable form to aid decision-making** - use summaries, diagrams and recommendations to help decision-making.

8. **Draw appropriate conclusions** - make sure your conclusions are fully supported by the relevant information and reasoned argument.

9. **Review your methods of obtaining information** - review your methods on a regular basis and improve them where necessary.

Recording and storing information

1. **Record information accurately** - check the quality of records.

2. **Record information in appropriate detail** - you will need to keep a different level of detail on information, depending on how significant it is and how you anticipate using it.

3. **Record and store information using accepted formats, systems and procedures** - your organisation may have developed formal procedures and systems for storing different types of information, both paper-based and on computer.

4. **Make sure you can retrieve information promptly when required** - consider how urgently the information may be needed.

5. **Review your methods for recording and storing information** - re-evaluate your methods, systems and procedures on a regular basis to check that they are as effective and efficient as possible.

6. **Introduce new methods of recording and storing information as needed** - regularly review whether the supply of information continues to meet requirements.

7. **Analyse and correct any breakdowns in the methods of recording and storing information** - when systems do breakdown, analyse the cause, and take action to ensure similar breakdowns do not re-occur.

8. **Comply with legal requirements** - ensure your systems for recording, storing and providing information meet legal requirements.

Managing Information

Forecasting trends and developments

1. **Base your forecasts on the best information available** - make sure you are using the best information given the constraints of time and cost.

2. **Make your forecasts of trends and developments at an appropriate time** - you will need to make some forecasts prior to planning; other developments may require forecasts to be regularly updated.

3. **Provide suitable quantitative information for decision making** - include in your forecasts sufficient quantitative information to allow you, and your colleagues, to be able to make decisions about allocating resources.

4. **State the assumptions underlying your forecasts** - clearly state your assumptions and the reasons for them.

5. **Clearly state the degree of certainty of your forecasts** - highlight those areas which are most at risk or where there is little evidence to support your forecast.

6. **Clearly illustrate the impact of trends and developments** - show how these trends will affect operations and the achievement of organisational objectives.

7. **Review your forecasts** - analyse the reasons for any inaccuracies in your forecasts, and use this information to improve future forecasts.

Using Information

Presenting information and advice

1. **Communicate** - seize opportunities to disseminate information and advice.

2. **Make sure your information is current, relevant and accurate** - prepare carefully what you are going to say and check it with colleagues or specialists.

3. **Check that your advice is consistent with organisational policy** - check with colleagues or specialists to ensure you are providing accurate advice.

4. **Support your advice** - where appropriate, provide reasoned argument and evidence to support your advice.

5. **Think about your audience** - put yourself in your audience's position, think what information they need, and present it in a manner, and at a level and pace which is appropriate.

6. **Check that your audience has understood** - ask questions, or use feedback, to check your audience has understood the information presented.

Meetings

This section is about leading and participating in meetings to make decisions.

The checklists will help you to:

- be clear about the purpose of the meeting and make sure its objectives are achieved
- prepare and make your contributions effectively
- encourage contributions from all participants
- take decisions.

This section covers:

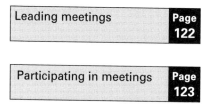

| Leading meetings | Page 122 |
| Participating in meetings | Page 123 |

Managing Information

Meetings

Leading meetings

1. **Be clear about the purpose of the meeting** - do not call a meeting if there is a better way to solve a problem or make a decision.

2. **Invite the appropriate people to attend** - only invite those people who have something to contribute or gain, but make sure you invite all the people necessary to take decisions.

3. **Allow time for preparation** - carefully prepare how you will lead the meeting and talk to other members; circulate papers in advance so everyone can be well prepared.

4. **Clearly state the purpose of the meeting at the outset** - check that all attendees share the same purpose.

5. **Allocate sufficient time** - set a fixed time for the meeting to begin and end and allocate time appropriately for each item under discussion.

6. **Encourage all attendees to contribute** - use questioning skills and individual encouragement to ensure all views are represented.

7. **Discourage unhelpful comments and digressions** - be firm, but sensitive, in asking attendees to keep to the purpose of the meeting.

8. **Summarise** - summarise the discussion at appropriate times and allocate action points at the end of each item.

9. **Take decisions** - make sure that decisions are within the meeting's authority, that they are accurately recorded and promptly communicated to those who need to know.

10. **Evaluate the meeting** - allow time at the end of the meeting to evaluate whether the purpose of the meeting has been effectively achieved.

Participating in meetings

1. **Prepare carefully** - get any papers or information in advance, and consult with others whom you are representing, so you can prepare how best to contribute to the meeting.

2. **Contribute effectively** - present your contributions clearly, accurately and at the appropriate time.

3. **Help to solve problems** - think about how you can help identify, clarify and come up with solutions to problems and help the meeting arrive at a valid decision.

4. **Keep to the point** - remember what the purpose of the meeting is and do not digress.

5. **Acknowledge the contributions and viewpoints of others** - acknowledge others' contributions and discuss these constructively, even if you disagree with them.

6. **Represent your group effectively** - if you are at the meeting as the representative of your organisation, department or team, make sure you fully represent their views, not just your own.

Managing Information

National Standards

What are National Standards?

National standards of performance, or 'occupational standards', have been developed for virtually all jobs in the UK today. The standards describe what people are expected to do in their jobs, and how they are expected to do them. There are, for example, occupational standards for retail staff, cooks, care workers, administrative staff, construction workers and those working in manufacturing and engineering industries.

The Management Standards, developed by the Management Charter Initiative (MCI) describe the standards of performance expected of managers and supervisors in their job roles. They also describe the knowledge base which managers need to be able to perform effectively. The Management Standards apply to all managers and supervisors, regardless of the sector in which they are working. Whilst the context may be different, the process of, say, counselling staff, budgeting or implementing a change programme will be similar in all industries.

The Management Standards are available at four different levels:

Standards	Qualification
Senior Management Standards	Under development
Middle Management Standards	NVQ/SVQ Level 5
First line Management Standards	NVQ/SVQ Level 4
Supervisory Management Standards	NVQ/SVQ Level 3

The Standards for Managing Quality describe the distinctive standards of performance expected of those with the specific responsibility to enhance the organisation's capability to improve its performance and develop excellence for its customers. They apply equally to those with the job title *Quality Manager* or *Quality Director* and to those with line management or functional management responsibilities who are clearly managing quality as a major part of their job.

The Management Standards and the Standards for Managing Quality, like all occupational standards, have been developed for assessment purposes, particularly assessment leading to National Vocational

Qualifications (NVQs) or Scottish Vocational Qualifications (SVQs). However, many organisations and their managers use the standards for a wide range of purposes, including recruitment and selection, training needs analysis, design of training programmes, performance review and appraisal, succession planning and promotion criteria. Organisations are now beginning to link them directly to quality initiatives such as BS EN ISO 9000, Total Quality Management and Investors in People.

The checklists for *Quality Management* are relevant to all those involved, either wholly or in part, with consistently meeting customers' requirements and continuously improving performance. They are based largely on the Standards for Managing Quality (see pages 130-131).

The checklists for *Operational Management* are relevant to all levels of management, although supervisors and first line managers may find they contribute to, rather than have full responsibility for, an activity. They are based mainly on the Middle Management Standards (see pages 132-133) and on other appropriate standards, such as those developed by the Customer Service Lead Body or the Training and Development Lead Body.

The links between the checklists and the different sets of standards are shown on pages 134-136.

National Vocational Qualifications

National Vocational Qualifications (NVQs), and Scottish Vocational Qualifications (SVQs), are certificates of employees' competence in their job roles. They are available to anyone who can prove that they are competent in the required units of the appropriate set of occupational standards.

There are five levels in the NVQ framework. Retail staff, for instance, can gain NVQs in retailing at levels 1-4, carpenters at level 2 or 3 and telesales staff at level 2.

The NVQ Framework

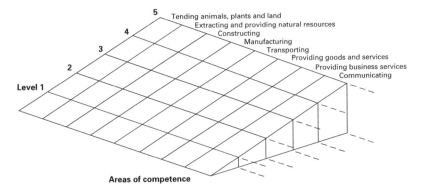

You can be awarded an NVQ or SVQ at level 3, 4 or 5 in management if you can satisfy the assessor that you are competent in the required units of the Management Standards at them appropriate level. If you can prove you are competent in all or some of the Standards for Managing Quality, you can be awarded *additional units* to your NVQ.

You will usually need to compile a portfolio of evidence supporting your claim to competence and submit this to an assessor at an Approved Centre. An NVQ or SVQ is not a training programme. It is a certificate of your competence to do your job as a quality manager. Of course, you may need some training and development to attain that level of competence.

If you are interested in gaining an NVQ or SVQ in management, or the additional units in managing quality, contact your local Approved Centre, details are available from MCI (address on page 143).

The NVQ process

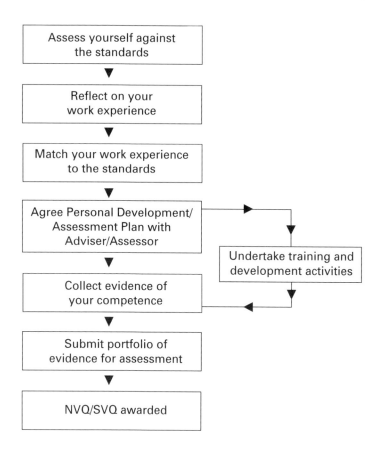

Assess yourself against the standards

▼

Reflect on your work experience

▼

Match your work experience to the standards

▼

Agree Personal Development/ Assessment Plan with Adviser/Assessor

▼

Undertake training and development activities

Collect evidence of your competence

▼

Submit portfolio of evidence for assessment

▼

NVQ/SVQ awarded

Standards for Managing Quality

The Standards for Managing Quality define the standard of performance required of those with specific responsibility for quality management. They form the basis of the checklists for *Quality Management*.

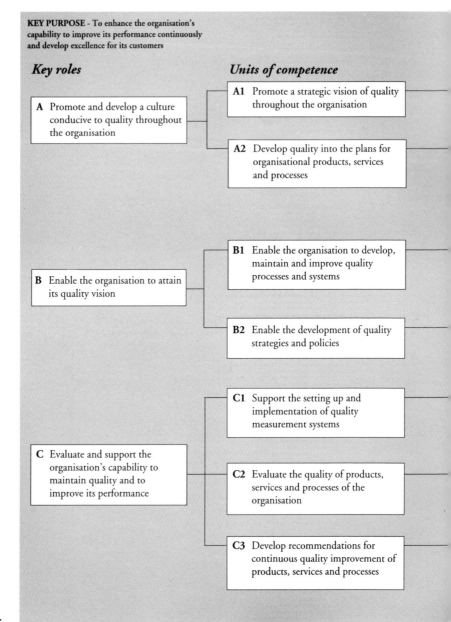

KEY PURPOSE - To enhance the organisation's capability to improve its performance continuously and develop excellence for its customers

Key roles

A Promote and develop a culture conducive to quality throughout the organisation

B Enable the organisation to attain its quality vision

C Evaluate and support the organisation's capability to maintain quality and to improve its performance

Units of competence

A1 Promote a strategic vision of quality throughout the organisation

A2 Develop quality into the plans for organisational products, services and processes

B1 Enable the organisation to develop, maintain and improve quality processes and systems

B2 Enable the development of quality strategies and policies

C1 Support the setting up and implementation of quality measurement systems

C2 Evaluate the quality of products, services and processes of the organisation

C3 Develop recommendations for continuous quality improvement of products, services and processes

Elements of competence

A1.1 Promote quality as a central force in the organisation's strategies for success

A1.2 Promote quality throughout the organisation and its customer and supplier networks

A2.1 Determine the quality of performance which customers require and expect

A2.2 Assess the organisation's performance against customer requirements and expectations

A2.3 Advise the organisation on the priority and value of improvements to performance

B1.1 Advise the organisation on the impact of working environments and processes on quality

B1.2 Advise and support the organisation on the implementation of plans to maintain and improve quality systems

B2.1 Support the organisation in the development of policies which will realise its vision of quality

B2.2 Identify strategies to implement quality policies

C1.1 Enable the organisation to design and develop measurement systems for the assessment of quality performance

C1.2 Support the collection, analysis and documentation of information relating to quality

C2.1 Design and implement evaluation systems and processes to monitor organisational performance

C2.2 Monitor and maintain the collection, analysis, documentation and storage of information on organisational performance

C3.1 Evaluate information relating to the quality of products, services and processes for their continuing suitability and effectiveness

C3.2 Advise on methods of continuous quality improvement for products, services and processes

National Standards

Middle Management Standards

The Middle Management Standards define the standard of performance required of operational managers with a broad range of responsibility. They form the basis of the checklists for *Operational Management*.

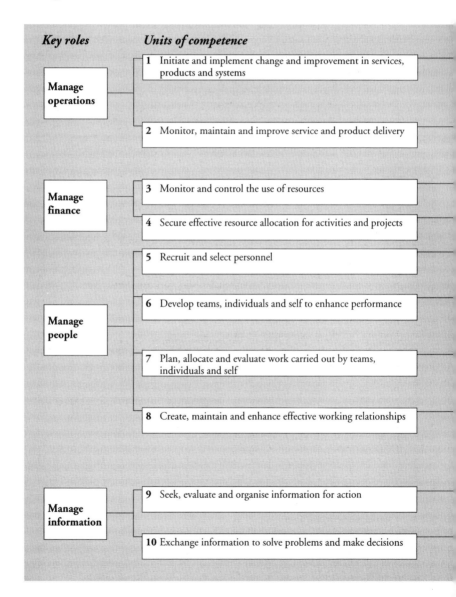

Key roles	Units of competence
Manage operations	**1** Initiate and implement change and improvement in services, products and systems
	2 Monitor, maintain and improve service and product delivery
Manage finance	**3** Monitor and control the use of resources
	4 Secure effective resource allocation for activities and projects
Manage people	**5** Recruit and select personnel
	6 Develop teams, individuals and self to enhance performance
	7 Plan, allocate and evaluate work carried out by teams, individuals and self
	8 Create, maintain and enhance effective working relationships
Manage information	**9** Seek, evaluate and organise information for action
	10 Exchange information to solve problems and make decisions

Elements of competence

1.1	Identify opportunities for improvement in services, products and systems
1.2	Evaluate proposed changes for benefits and disadvantages
1.3	Negotiate and agree the introduction of change
1.4	Implement and evaluate changes to services, products and systems
1.5	Introduce, develop and evaluate quality assurance systems

2.1	Establish and maintain the supply of resources into the organisation/department
2.2	Establish and agree customer requirements
2.3	Maintain and improve operations against quality and functional specifications
2.4	Create and maintain the necessary conditions for productive work activity

3.1	Control costs and enhance value
3.2	Monitor and control activities against budgets

4.1	Justify proposals for expenditure on projects
4.2	Negotiate and agree budgets

5.1	Define future personnel requirements
5.2	Determine specifications to secure quality people
5.3	Assess and select candidates against team and organisational requirements

6.1	Develop and improve teams through planning and activities
6.2	Identify, review and improve development activities for individuals
6.3	Develop oneself within the job role
6.4	Evaluate and improve the development processes used

7.1	Set and update work objectives for teams and individuals
7.2	Plan activities and determine work methods to achieve objectives
7.3	Allocate work and evaluate teams, individuals and self against objectives
7.4	Provide feedback to teams and individuals on their performance

8.1	Establish and maintain the trust and support of one's subordinates
8.2	Establish and maintain the trust and support of one's immediate manager
8.3	Establish and maintain relationships with colleagues
8.4	Identify and minimise interpersonal conflict
8.5	Implement disciplinary and grievance procedures
8.6	Counsel staff

9.1	Obtain and evaluate information to aid decision making
9.2	Forecast trends and developments which affect objectives
9.3	Record and store information

10.1	Lead meetings and group discussions to solve problems and make decisions
10.2	Contribute to discussions to solve problems and make decisions
10.3	Advise and inform others

National Standards

133

Links between the Checklists and the Standards

Quality Management Checklists	Standards for Managing Quality
Promoting the Importance of Quality	
Promoting the strategic role of quality	A1.1
Promoting quality throughout your organisation	A1.2
Promoting Quality in Organisational Plans	
Identifying customers' quality requirements	A2.1
Assessing your organisation's quality performance	A2.2
Advising on improvements	A2.3
Supporting Quality Policies and Strategies	
Supporting the development of quality policies	B2.1
Identifying strategies to implement quality policies	B2.2
Supporting Quality Processes and Systems	
Advising on the impact of working environments and processes on quality	B1.1
Advising on the implementation of quality systems	B1.2
Supporting Quality Measurement	
Supporting the design and development of quality measurement systems	C1.1
Supporting the collection, analysis and documentation of information relating to quality	C1.2
Evaluating Quality	
Designing and implementing evaluation systems	C2.1
Managing information on organisational performance	C2.2
Supporting Continuous Improvement	
Evaluating the quality of products, services and processes	C3.1
Advising on continuous quality improvement	C3.2

National Standards

Links between the Checklists and the Standards

Operational Management Checklists	Middle Management	First Line Management	Supervisory Management
Meeting Customer Needs			
Establishing and agreeing customer requirements	2.2		
Maintaining supplies	2.1		
Maintaining a productive work environment	2.4	1.2	1.2
Meeting customer specifications	2.3	1.1	1.1
Solving problems for customers			
Managing Change			
Identifying opportunities for improvements	1.1		
Assessing the pros and cons of change	1.2	2.1	
Negotiating and agreeing the introduction of change	1.3		
Implementing and evaluating changes	1.4	2.2	
Quality Assurance			
Assuring quality	1.5		
Time Management			
Managing your time			
Personnel Planning			
Planning human resource requirements	5.1	4.1	3.1
Drawing up job specifications	5.2		
Assessing and selecting staff	5.3	4.2	3.1
Making staff redundant			
Developing Teams and Individuals			
Developing teams	6.1	5.1	4.1
Developing individuals	6.2	5.2	4.1
Developing yourself	6.3	5.3	4.4
Coaching			4.2
Mentoring			
Evaluating and improving training and development	6.4	5.2	4.3
Managing Teams and Individuals			
Planning work	7.2	6.2	5.1
Allocating work	7.3	6.3	5.2
Setting objectives	7.1	6.1	5.2
Giving feedback	7.4	6.4	5.3
Working Relationships			
Building a relationship with your manager	8.2	7.2	6.2
Building relationships with staff	8.1	7.1	6.1
Building relationships with colleagues	8.3	7.3	6.1
Minimising conflict	8.4	7.4	6.3
Managing Problems with Staff			
Counselling	8.6	7.6	
Implementing grievance and disciplinary procedures	8.5	7.5	6.4
Firing staff			

Continued

National Standards

Operational Management Checklists

	Middle Management	First Line Management	Supervisory Management
Equal Opportunities			
Promoting equal opportunities			
Encouraging diversity and fair working practices			
Managing Budgets			
Preparing budgets	4.1	3.1	2.1
Negotiating and agreeing budgets	4.2		
Monitoring budgets	3.2	3.2	2.2
Cost Control			
Controlling costs	3.1	3.2	2.2
Using Information			
Obtaining and evaluating information	9.1	8.1	7.1
Recording and storing information	9.3	8.2	7.1
Forecasting trends and developments	9.2		
Presenting information and advice	10.3	9.3	7.2
Meetings			
Leading meetings	10.1	9.1	
Participating in meetings	10.2	9.2	

Keywords Index

Accidents
accident procedure 56
costing 36
reduction 16,22

Advice & Guidance
presenting 119
providing 23,29-31,36-37, 44-45

Agreements
budgets 109
change 62
customers 54
records of 62
suppliers 55

Analysis
of requirements 20
cost-benefit analysis 22,45
of information 33,35,37,44

Aspirations
of individuals 89

Assessment
change 22,61
facilitating 82
organisation's quality
  performance 21
recruitment 74
self-assessment 80,89

Assumptions
budgets 109
forecasts 118

Audience
feedback 119
presentations 119

Authority
budgets 110,112
limits of 87

Benchmarking 21

Benefits (see also evaluating)
of quality 15,16,22,25,26, 35,36,45

Briefing
on work 87

Budgets
agreeing 109
monitoring 110
negotiating 109
preparing 108

Champions 17

Change
effects of 22,61
implementation 63
managing change 59-63
obstacles to 22
pros and cons 61

Coaching 81

Commitment
to equal opportunities 102
to quality assurance 26,66

Communication
with candidates 74
with colleagues 62-63,66
with customers 54,58,66
with staff 66,75,99

Competitor
activity 55
comparing
  performance 20-21

Conflict
external 26
minimising 87,95
with colleagues 94

Conformance
quality 22

Constraints 22,45

Consultation
with colleagues 58,72,73,119
with manager 92
with staff 66,72,73,75,78,86, 88,93,108
with teams 78,86

Contingency
planning 68,108
allowances 109

Contracts 20

Control
systems 29-30

Corrective action
expenditure 110,112
income 110
operations 57
quality 43-44

Cost (see also Expenditure)
analysing 22
control 111-112
cost-benefit analysis 22,45
cost-effectiveness 63,78,79
costing systems 22
human resources 72
savings 16

Counselling
personal problems 98
redundancy 75

Criteria
for system design 36
prioritisation 22
selection 74

Culture
quality 13

Customers
charter 20
communication 54,58
feedback 20-21,54
needs, requirements 19-21,53,54,66
problems 58
quality 15-16,25-26,39-41
satisfaction 16

Debriefing
after training 83

Decision-making
change 61
decision-makers 15-17, 27
independent 82
meetings 122
time management 68

Delegating
time management 68

Development (see also Training & Development)
identification of needs 78-81

Digressions
avoiding 123
controlling 68
discouraging 122

Direction
degrees of 86

Discipline
procedures 99-100, 103

Discrimination
challenging 103

Discussing problems and concerns
with manager 92
with staff 93-95

Dismissal 75,100

Disruptions
minimising 57

Diversity
of working styles 103

Documentation
system 26,30-31,33,35,
37,39-41

Employees
motivation 16
quality 15-16,26

Encouragement
contributions 122
feedback 89
mentoring 82
performance 88

Environment
working 23,29,30

Equipment
availability 56
developments 60
maintenance 56

Estimates
income 108
expenditure 108

Equal Opportunities
action plan 102
diversity 102
fair working practices 103
policy 102
procedures 74
promoting equal
opportunities 102
recruitment 74
redundancy 75

Evaluating
changes 63
equal opportunities 102
information 116
meetings 122
performance 89
quality 33,39-40,43-45, 66
reports 36
systems 39,40
training &
development 83

Expenditure
budgets 107-110
estimates 108
monitoring 110
phasing 110
variances 110

Experience
learning from   54,60,61,63,83, 87,95,99,108

Facilitating
learning   82
assessment   82

Feedback
from customers   57
from others   37,80
to individuals   57,88,89,103
to learners   81-82
to teams   57,89

Finance
managing   105-112

Firing staff   100

Forecasting
trends and developments   118

Friction
minimising   78

Grievance
procedure   99

Human Resource
planning   71-75

Income
budgets   108-110
estimates   108
monitoring   110
variances   110

Improvements
advising on   13,19,22
continuous   17,33,40,43,45
performance   13,21,44
quality systems   29-31

Inconsistencies
internal   26

Information
about customer problems   58
about developments   60
about grievance & disciplinary procedures   99
about threats & opportunities   92
evaluating   116
managing information   113-123
obtaining   116
on budgets   108-109
on costs   112
on customer needs   54

on performance   41
on quality   17,27,30-31, 36,39-40,44
planning   72
presenting information   62,119
qualitative   20
quantitative   20
recording   117
storing   117

Interruptions
controlling   68

Involvement (see consultation)

Job specifications   73

Knowledge
requirements   73

Law (legal requirements)
agreements   54
conflicts at work   95
equal opportunities   74,102-103
grievance & disciplinary procedures   99
health & safety   20, 30
information   41
job specifications   73
recruitment & selection   74
redundancy   75
work methods   86
workplace   30,56

Learning
style   81

Maintenance
equipment   56

Management Charter Initiative (MCI)   6,126-127,143

Materials
developments   60
supplies   55,56

Measurement
quality   33,35-36
performance   36,39-40

Meetings
leading   122
participating   123

Mentoring   82

Misconduct (gross)   100

Mission
of organisation   16,26

Monitoring
budgets 110
changes 63
improvements 45
information 44
operations 57
procedures 31

National Standards 125-136

National Vocational
Qualifications
(NVQs) 6,126-129

National Council for
Vocational Qualifications
(NCVQ) 143

Negotiation
budgets 109
change 62
customers 54
for resources 40

Networks
developing 116

Non-conformance
quality 22

Objectives
achievement 88
development 78-80,83
individual 68,73,81-82,88,92
learning 81-82
of evaluation 40
organisational 86-87,95

Operational management 47-123

Participation (see also Commitment and
Consultation)
change 62

People
managing 69-103

Performance
assessing 13,21
comparing with others 20-21
encouraging 88-89
improving 13,21-22,44
measurement 26,36,39-40
organisational 41
quality 13,21
review 89

Personnel
planning 71-75

Plans
contingencies 68
implementing change 62
implementing
quality systems 31
operational 57
organisational 13,19-22
personnel 71-75
presenting 62-63
time 68
work 86

Policy
advice 92,119
counselling 98
customer problems 58
health and safety 26
organisational 20,27
quality 23,25-27
redundancy 75

Preparation
for meetings 122-123

Presenting
advice 119,123
budgets 108
information 16, 119,123
plans 63,72

Price
supplies 55

Priorities
time management 68

Problems
counselling 98
customers 58
discussing 92-93,95
obstacles to change 60,63
quality 36,40,43-44
solving 58,122-123
staff 97-100

Procedures
accident 56
appeals 75
customer problems 58
disciplinary 99-100,103
grievance 99
improvements 60
monitoring 31
quality 66
recruitment &
selection 74
redundancy 75

Processes
of organisation 19,30
quality 21,23,26,29,30,
33,36,39-41,43-45

Products
delivering 19,26,29
provision of 53-55
quality of 21,26,29,33,
39-41,43-45

Productivity 56

Promises
to colleagues 94
to staff 93

Promoting & publicising
improvements 16
quality 13,15-17

Proposals
presenting 92

Quality
assurance 65-66
awareness 17
British Quality Award 10
BS 5750 10
BS 7850 10
BS EN ISO 9000 10
European Quality
Award 10
improvements 60
inspection 21
performance 13,19,21
policy 23,25-27
practices 16
Quality Management 7-45
requirements 13,19-20
service 55
standards 10,16,19-22,
26-27,30-31,36,41,44
strategy 15-16,23,25-27
systems 8,16,23,26,29,31
Total Quality
Management
(TQM) 10
vision 21,23,25-27

Recognition
of achievement 89
of ideas, views,
contributions 93,123

Recommendations
improvements 43,45,59-63,112
firing staff 100
from auditors 36
grievance &
disciplinary
procedures 99
recruitment &
selection 74
quality 27,33,36, 66
working conditions 56

Records
change 62
conflicts 95
customers 54
department 56
expenditure 112
feedback 89
grievance &
disciplinary
procedures 99
information 117
operation 57
quality 40,44
recruitment &
selection 74
suppliers 55
working environment 30

Recruitment & selection 74

Redundancy 75

Relationships
with colleagues 94
with manager 92
with mentees 82
with staff 93
with those
responsible for
quality 30-31,40

Representing
others 123

Research (see also Review)
customer needs 54

Resources
developments 60
effective use 30,40,45,57,
63,66,78,79
supplies 56,57
implications 22,27

Responsibility
individual 87,95
for quality 31
job specifications 73
team 87,95

Results (see Evaluating)

Review
change 63
customer problems 58
development plans 78-79
forecasts 118
information
requirements 116
information storage 117
job descriptions 73
mentoring 82
organisational
performance 89
progress 68
suppliers 55

Risk
assessment 22

Sampling 40

Satisfaction of customers 58,66

Schedules 57

**Scottish Vocational
    Qualifications**
    (SVQs) 6, 126-129

SCOTVEC 143

Selection
of staff 74

Services
delivering 19,26,29
provision of 54-55
quality 19,21,29,33,
    39-41,43-45

Skills
coaching 81
developing 77-83
identification of needs 72

Special needs
costs 72
identifying 102
working environment 56

Specialists
access 87
advice 119
equal opportunities 103
grievance &
    disciplinary
    procedures 99
job specifications 73
training &
    development 78

Specifications
quality 20,31

Staff involvement (see consultation)

Standards
BS 5750 10
BS7850 10
BS EN ISO 9000 10
for Managing Quality 6, 126-131
of behaviour 95
of organisation 19
of work 95
Management Standards 126-134
quality 16,19-22,26-27,
    29-31,36,41,44

Stereotyping
discouraging 103

Strategy 13,15-16,23,25,27
Strengths
individual 79,102
self 80
team 78

Summarising
action points 122

Supervision
of work 87

Suppliers
quality 15,22,25,27,39-41

Supply
consistency 16
disruption 22
procurement strategies 26

Support
for continuous
    improvement 43
for learning 82
for manager 92
for mentees 82
for quality 25-26,29,31,35-37,45
for staff 93

Surveys 20

Team
development 78,80
management 85-89
qualities required 72

Technology
change 60

Threats
information about 92

Time
efficient use 67-68
for development 80
for others 93-94
management 67-68
meetings 122

Training & Development
costs 72
equal opportunities 102
evaluating 83
individuals 79
opportunities in work 87
plans 77-80,83
quality 26
redundancy 75

self 80
teams 78
use of equipment 56

Tools & techniques
quality management 36-37
assessment 40

Understanding
checking 63,66,87,88,93

Value
added value 22
supplies 55
valuing systems 22

Values
of organisation 16, 20, 27

Vision
of organisation 16-17,21,23,25-27,29

Weaknesses
individual 79
self 80
team 78

Work
allocation 87,95
briefing 87
environment 56
methods 86
supervision 87

Useful Addresses

Management Charter Initiative
Russell Square House
10-12 Russell Square
London WC1B 5BZ
Tel: 0171 872 9000
Fax: 0171 872 9099

National Council for Vocational Qualifications
222 Euston Road
London NW1 2BZ
Tel: 0171 387 9898
Fax: 0171 387 0978

SCOTVEC
Hanover House
24 Douglas Street
Glasgow G2 7NQ
Tel: 0141 248 7900
Fax: 0141 242 2244

The Institute of Quality Assurance
61 Southwark Street
London SE1 1SB
Tel: 0171 401 7227
Fax: 0171 401 2725